Aude

Rolland

Enjoy Reading

27/06/2015

A Mother's Debt

THE TRUE STORY OF AN AFRICAN ORPHAN

TALENT CHIOMA
MUNDY-CASTLE

authorHOUSE®

AuthorHouse™
1663 Liberty Drive
Bloomington, IN 47403
www.authorhouse.com
Phone: 1-800-839-8640

Published by AuthorHouse   11/17/2012

ISBN: 978-1-4772-1834-1 (sc)
ISBN: 978-1-4772-1833-4 (hc)
ISBN: 978-1-4772-1875-4 (e)

CONTENTS

DEDICATION

I have written this account of my life with my five children and all my grandchildren in mind. Without their support, from which I draw my strength, I would not have had the courage to put pen to paper. The debt I inherited from my mother has been repaid with the help of subsequent generations, faith, hope and charity.

This is for:

Chinedum Gloria
Osinachim Paul,
Nnamudi Godwin,
Chiweuba Andrew,
Oluchineke Emma,
their children and, Mundy-Castle
May my God Bless you all, Thank God

ACKNOWLEDGEMENTS

Many years have flown away and I continually surprise myself that I am still here to tell the world that our lives are in our own hands. I firmly believe that the key is to play the cards as they are dealt, without any negativity or doubt, since these only serve to cloud the issues and alter the outcome. I did not know my mother and was with my father only for a short period, so I can only thank them for the inherited genes that have enabled me to be who I am today.

As I was much younger than them I did not know my eight brothers well, only one of whom survived the terrible Nigeria/Biafran civil war. Their contribution to the Igbo cause was immense, even in defeat, and they paid the ultimate sacrifice for their beliefs. I am privileged to have also been able to take part in that struggle. We all fought in the war, but never together, and I have no knowledge of how each one died. They just didn't return, like a million others. Silently, they were wiped off the world's stage, and quickly forgotten in the chaos of a country awaking from a nightmare.

Although there were many hard times my children were always there for me, eventually giving my life some purpose though, at times, I found it hard to understand what God's plan was. Gloria, Paul, Godwin, Andy and Emma grew up under my strict interpretations of discipline and, in turn, kept an eye on me as they each reached their own point of realisation. They came to understand that the single most important factor missing from my early life was a caring and loving atmosphere and, in turn, made it their business to redress that omission. I am much calmer now having established that, at last, love is flowing into me. There is no greater love than that emanating from one's own bloodline. I thank them for being there.

A vital part of my life was reshaped by a giant among men. My husband, Lister, taught me that there was no such thing as terminal mistrust. He planted in me the seed that I could be a 'Lady of Substance' by gradually calming my anger and making me aware that there was much good in the world. What he brought into my life is immeasurable and my gratitude to him knows no boundary. He took me and my three children on, gave me two more, and educated us all to the highest standards possible. He also gave me good feelings for men whom I had come to despise.

I am respectful of all those who contributed to my upbringing, good or bad, since everything happens for a reason. I have mellowed greatly over the years and, in hindsight, can see that there was much laudable purpose for many, but not all, of the actions of the people who crossed my path. I would single out for particular attention my stepmother, Jemima, who constantly appears in my story as a tyrannical character. In fact, it was the result of a clash of personalities between us and I have come to the conclusion that without her presence, at strategic moments in my life, I would have been much weaker. I now firmly believe that, during our battles, my individuality was forming and this gave me the strength of character and purpose that I would need to carry me forward. Although, given the option, I would not have chosen her for the role, she was truly my substitute mother and I ask forgiveness for any pain I caused her. I like to think she would feel the same if she were still here today.

Finally my heartfelt thanks go to Michael Rodney Guise who was the driving force in the completion of this book. He supported me with words of encouragement and sympathy while I was re-living the darkest corners of my past. Without this support I would not have had the courage to go to these places which I had not visited for years. I cannot sufficiently express my gratitude to him for taking this on and I know that it was just as painful for him.

I hope my story can help others, especially those unfortunate children in similar circumstances. I thank my God that I am here now to be able to pass on my experiences.

Talent Mundy-Castle

CHAPTER 1
The Morning of My Life

It was as though the diminishing strength of my mother, Grace, as her life ebbed away during the days following my birth, was imbuing my body with the power I would need for the rigours of my own journey. My entrance into this world, just as she was exiting it, was as unconventional as my life was to become. It is only now at the age of 55 that I can finally summon the strength I need to recount the events that followed.

It was June 1954 and it was planned that I should be born in the village of Ezuhu Nguru, Aboh, Mbaise in former Eastern Nigeria—my father, Jonathan Oparaji, was elated at the prospect of at least one of his and Grace's children originating in his home town, a dream he had long nurtured. His leave had fitted in perfectly with the projected birth date.

A few days before my arrival my mother, Grace, had been collecting vegetables in my grandmother's garden when a large snake appeared and wound itself around her waist. The villagers raced to the scene on hearing her screams but could do little to help as the reptile was tightly coiled around her and her unborn child and, in her state, they could have caused more damage by attempting a rescue.

My father, Jonathan, had driven his Morris Minor to the market square to buy meat when a villager raced up to tell him what was happening. He quickly drove to the scene and to everyone's amazement the snake, startled by the sound of the car door slamming, fell from my mother, who then collapsed, unconscious. On the spot where the snake fell an egg had appeared and spilt into two segments, revealing nothing, completely dry. My father and the villagers were unable to comprehend what this meant and it was decided by majority that the pagan gods should be consulted. My paternal grandfather suggested that my mother's father, a pagan, should be called in to ask the gods for an explanation of the meaning for this distressing incident. A solution to Grace's condition could then be worked out. However, my father, a strong willed man and a Christian, would hear none of this and ordered Grace to be lifted into his car so that he could drive her to the Shell Oil Hospital at Port Harcourt.

On arrival at the hospital Grace, who was still unconscious, was rushed into an emergency ward where she clung on to life until, two or three days later, she fell into labour, and I was born in perfect health. Jonathan was pleased at this development but my mother was still precariously balanced between life and death and the hospital doctors were of the opinion that death was the most likely outcome. They were unable to explain to him the cause of her grave state so Jonathan made the decision to try the pagan solution that had originally been recommended by Grace's father (based on the assumption that the reason was spiritual, not medical). So he had Grace taken back to Nguru in a desperate attempt to save her, leaving me alone in Port Harcourt hospital.

My natural parents Jonathan and Grace Oparaji. I never
knew my mother, and my father died when I was 5.

Grace was put to bed in her husband's house and, after Jonathan had explained what he wanted, my maternal grandfather went to see the native doctors who came immediately to see my mother. They recommended that, since she was so near to death, someone close to her should be prepared to try and bring her back. This would entail 'killing' the chosen rescuer by traditional methods; i.e. pouring a form of anesthetic into his nose until he was unconscious. The person selected for this task was my mother's younger brother, Humphrey, who was a teacher and a Christian. Despite his beliefs he unhesitatingly agreed to this, although my father stipulated that he would not accept Humphrey's death as the price for saving his wife's life. He ominously warned the native doctors that if Humphrey was not brought back then someone else would suffer.

Humphrey was then given the anesthetic and quickly succumbed. However, after two hours he had not come round and the native doctors became worried, especially since Jonathan had threatened them with reprisals if anything happened to him, but eventually, to everyone's relief, his eyes suddenly opened looking startled as reality replaced dreams. At this point Humphrey takes up the story:

> "I was walking along a road behind Grace and some other people, none of whom I recognised. They were approaching a gate ahead of them when, suddenly, she turned round and looked straight at me."

"She shouted, 'Go back, Go back!! If I get hold of you I'll give you a beating!'

"But I continued to follow until Grace, without further warning, turned again and ran towards me. I was caught by the swiftness of this move and she hit me hard on the head and I fell".

"The next thing I knew was coughing and waking up in front of the doctors and Jonathan. I told them that I had been unsuccessful in bringing my sister back and that she hadn't wanted to come with me".

Grace had died before Humphrey recovered but my father was angry at the length of time he had been unconscious and the villagers had to protect the native doctors from Jonathan's wrath. Eventually he calmed down and accepted the inevitable.

3

No logical explanation was offered by anyone for the snake episode and Grace's Christian funeral duly took place. This was her last journey and the beginning of mine.

My father's pain at the loss of his wife was so great that he could not bring himself to take me out of hospital. Along with thousands of other men from British Colonial Nigeria he had uncomplainingly fought with the Allies in Burma during World War II and, for unknown reasons, had retired to Ireland with his family after being released from service at the cessation of hostilities in 1946.

My parents (both of Eastern Nigerian origin) had 6 sons born in Ireland, and on their return to Africa Jonathan was contracted to run a businessman's club in Abonima, Kalagbari, in Rivers State. My parents had 2 more sons, and then the routine changed—the girl for whom Grace had yearned finally arrived, but with tragic consequences for both of us. I would undergo the long drawn out trauma of a childhood dogged by the twin reputations of being both my mother's murderer and a child witch. Added to this would be the stigma of being an orphan when, a few short years later, my father would die. This was a horrendous burden for a child to carry in Nigeria and the practice of child witchery still exists to this day. Without parents I would belong to nobody and become the whipping child and slave of any relative in my compound who thought fit to use me for their own ends. The only alternative for children caught in the horrors of this barbaric practice was to run away. But, of course, this could result in repercussions which might be even worse.

Before my father died I was happily innocent of my sinister status since he loved me and kept me protected from those who had only hate in their hearts for the likes of me. One of my earliest memories was the visit of Dick Tiger (the famous Nigerian light heavyweight world champion boxer, and active supporter of the Biafran independence movement) to my father's club for a match. I became fascinated, and still am, with the sport of boxing.

The account of my mother's death was told to me much later by both my grandfathers who each lived to be over 100. My paternal grandfather was thought to have lived to be 123, and my mother's father to 101.

I was christened Irene Chioma. The choice of Irene was my father's and, although he appeared to have borne no animosity towards me for

Grace's death, he had had no option but to leave me in the hospital in the care of nurses. This was mainly due to the fact that both my grandmothers, who would normally have looked after me, were dead. He visited me regularly in the hospital and, subsequently, in the adjoining orphanage where I lived for my first three years. I remember these occasions and of being led out by the nurses to meet him. I recall how gentle he was and how attached I felt to him. I always felt empty for some time after he left. In fact, I had many visitors but was uncertain of who they all were.

When I was three years old my father remarried, to Jemima, and claimed me back from the orphanage. From this point in time my memories are my own and not events recounted to me by others. I was given a farewell party at the orphanage and I remember the strange feeling of assuming all the nurses were my mothers. Now Jemima had come to take me away and I accepted this as my father always made sure I was treated well.

I initially thought Jemima was my real mother. She was extremely beautiful but very strict and domineering, which I came to interpret as wickedness. I was punished with beatings and had pepper rubbed in my eyes and private parts, particularly viciously when I wet the bed. However, this only happened when my father was at work. When he returned I told him of these occurrences and began to wonder if she really was my mother. My father tried confronting Jemima but she denied everything until, on one occasion, he unexpectedly returned to the house to find me screaming with pain from the pepper treatment. He then realised I had been telling the truth, but the outcome of this was to cause increasing friction between them.

Therefore, I was alternatively happy and unhappy, depending on who was in the house. The abiding memory I have of my father, as he tried to comfort me, is of him playing gramophone records (His Master's Voice) and asking me to dance for him. His favourite song was 'Irene, goodnight Irene, I'll see you in my dreams.' That has lived with me over the years and when I hear it now the feeling of loss is still vivid. A promise he often made to me, as we talked together, was to send me to Ireland for further studies when I was older. However, he wasn't able to fulfil that promise, although I did eventually visit Ireland but under very different circumstances to those he had implanted in my mind.

My life continued in this fractured fashion until in 1959, when I was 5, my father suddenly died. Some say he was poisoned, which is a popular way of getting rid of enemies in Nigeria. It is often done, not by direct methods, but spiritually (i.e. ju ju) and is thought to still account for a number of deaths today.

When he became ill he was admitted to hospital and, as was the practice, my stepmother went to look after him. I and my three stepbrothers were sent to Jemima's village, Amuzi, Mbaise. to be looked after by her parents. We lived there for about 6 months when, one morning, an uncle (Christian) arrived on a bicycle and asked my brothers and me to go outside while he talked with my step-grandparents. My grandmother then came outside and told us to get ready to go back to Nguru, my own village, without any explanation. At this point, on seeing the expressions on their faces I suspected that something unpleasant was about to be revealed. Then I asked my uncle if my father was back in the village.

He replied, tersely, "No problem, let's go", and loaded us on to his bicycle (me on the crossbar and my stepbrothers behind the saddle on the carrier frame) for the four mile journey to my home. He wouldn't directly answer my constant questioning and didn't seem to want to engage in conversation. I became anxious and started to experience the gnawing anticipation of impending bad news.

My stepmother Jemima and my father Jonathan.

About a mile from my home there were increasing numbers of people on the road walking towards my village. Some were openly crying and some had their hands on their heads indicating that a tragedy had occurred. I tried to engage my uncle again, to get him to tell me what was happening, but he would only say that I should wait till we got home. The closer we got to my home the more congested the road became and eventually it was impossible to ride further due to the density of people. We dismounted and my uncle pushed us through the crowd and, as we did so, I heard people saying, "That's his daughter", and then I knew the worst. The tension within in me burst and I broke down screaming as the truth dawned on me. People were holding me and trying to restrain me from hurting myself. I was inconsolable.

Gradually I became aware of the voice of my grandfather, my father's father and the village chief, who I think was 110 at that time and the only person, other than my father, whom I genuinely loved. He was shouting in his frail voice for me to be brought to him. I got to his side and, although I was still distraught, I was aware of how fragile he was and managed to calm down. He said he would explain everything if I stopped crying and that he would then take me to see my father for the last time. This confused me, but since my trust in him was so strong I felt the tension and anxiety within me lessen.

I was composed now and he told me to hold on to him tightly, more so to steady him and, with others around to give support, we walked towards his house. At the doorway the others stopped and my grandfather and I entered alone and proceeded to his living room.

Suddenly, this was the moment where all the uncertainty vanished and I was confronted with the hard undeniable truth. My father's body lay on a ceremonial bed; his eyes were covered with a white band and the nose and mouth were stuffed with cotton wool. I started to lose my composure and turned to my grandfather to ask him why he had left me. What made the situation worse was the knowledge within me that there were so few people to whom I felt close that I couldn't afford to lose any of them. In fact my grandfather was now one of the last people left in whom I had any confidence. This was a characteristic of mine as, although I was part of a large family of mothers, brothers, uncles and aunties, I was always conscious of the lack of deep and close warmth from other human beings, especially family members. I suppose that this is what has made me steel myself against the adversities of life and to form intense feelings, good or bad, towards others.

After a short time my grandfather gently guided me out of the room to his bedroom where he tried to console me. I was crying silently in my grief and trying to comprehend what all this meant for me. I had not thought of the effect of his son's death on him but gradually became aware of him talking quietly. He said that my father was the most successful of his sixteen children and that he had never expected to be saying farewell to him this way.

As he spoke I started to think of the past and the times when my father and I had travelled from Port Harcourt to Nguru to visit him. He had always made sure that I was given palm wine, explaining that this was a traditional substitute for mother's milk when this is not available, as it was in my case. I was only ever given this by my grandfather and it stopped when he died for no one else seemed to follow this tradition.

After my father's funeral Jemima became even more domineering towards me. She persecuted me mercilessly with remarks such as, "Now that you are no longer the princess you'll have to behave and eat as we villagers do." This was a reference to the fact that we were now poor, since my father's money had been widely dispersed to the more powerful family members, and very little had been left for us. Additionally, I was the only one of my parent's children left at home; all my brothers had long gone: to boarding school, military training, or work. They rarely came home and I knew very little about them. Consequently there was nobody of my own blood or age from which to seek any sympathy. I remember the rejection and the label given to me, of 'Spiritual Child'—a convenient description for someone who had been responsible for their own mother's death. A debt from which I could only be released by eventually becoming a mother myself. But before that could happen I had a journey of nightmare proportions to travel. After all, this was Africa where a debt such as this was not tolerated, and almost impossible to repay.

My paternal grandfather died shortly after my father's departure. They put his age at 123 on his headstone which conflicted with my understanding that he had been 110 when my father died. This goes to show how unreliable record keeping was in those days. The wide variations in timings is due to the fact that dates, especially in rural areas, were based on the individual memories of significant events (storms, wars, etc.) which happen at stages in a person's life. I had been invited to be a bridesmaid at my Uncle Humphrey's wedding (The same Humphrey who was sent, unsuccessfully, to bring my mother back from the gates of heaven) and during the ceremony someone told me that my grandfather wanted to see me in his house. I had known that he was sick before I left the family compound to go to the church so, when I was told he was asking for me, I hurried back and found him alone in his house lying on his bed, one leg on the bed and the other with the foot on the floor by the fireplace. This was a typical position he often took up.

I called to him 3 times, "Dede, Dede, Dede," and he opened his eyes.

"It's me, Nwaolorondu," I said. This was his name for me and means, 'You have come to live.' No one ever called me that again after he died.

"Touch my hands," he said feebly, which I did, "Touch my leg. You can see they are very cold now."

I could hardly hear what he was saying and I lifted his leg on to the bed to make him more comfortable. At that moment I instantly recognised the similarity with my father's final laying out after his death.

"Dede, Dede, Dede," I called again, more anxiously this time.

He opened his eyes and asked me to lift down 3 boxes from the termite stands under which was a vaseline bottle, containing keys.

"Keep the bottle and make your demands," he whispered, "Whatever you want shall be given to you."

I was unsure what he meant, and repeated, "Dede, Dede, Dede."

His voice was becoming very faint and, struggling with his words, he managed to say,

"Whenever you're in need pick up a stone, put it on your heart, and help will be provided."

These were the last words he spoke to me. I had always been fearful of the dark and the deaths of others. I went to the extent of taking long routes round spots where people had died. My grandfather knew this and had tried to help me to counter this fear over the years. I knew that he was preparing me for his departure and that now was his time. I became afraid and, unable to rouse him further, ran out of the room to find his brother (also extremely old) as all the younger family members were at the wedding.

When I found the brother he would only say, "Leave him alone, he's been like that for days."

After a while one of my grandfather's sons came in and I told him what had happened. He went to look and came back to confirm he was dead and, telling me not to cry, explained that he was a king and no one should cry singly.

"Everyone should cry simultaneously on the beat of a drum to signify that the big tree has fallen."

This was a very significant moment in my life as I felt that there was now no one left who could protect me against the dangers of the world. I was now truly alone and unwanted, exposed and without any close older relatives to respect and depend upon. In the absence of my parents all the major figures in my pre-teenage years were gone. All my brothers had left the family compound to attend boarding school or work.

Additionally, I would now have a problem getting enough to eat. Jemima had virtually excluded me from her feeding plans, unless there was anything left over after her own children had eaten, and my grandfather had known this. Consequently, he always ordered more than he needed so that there was enough for me. Even if it was not sufficient for both of us he would forego his meal so that I could eat. The implications of being a child witch were intensifying and, as a result, I was becoming feral. I was going to have to grow up fast and take control of my destiny if I was to have any chance of a meaningful life.

CHAPTER 2

Working for Life

Shortly after my father died in 1959 his widow, Jemima, had started taking temporary work on local farms. She took me and her sons (my stepbrothers) along to help. It was little short of slave labour but I did recognise that it was necessary for survival since Jemima had no money. It is unclear what had happened to my father's wealth and nobody has been able to satisfactorily explain where it went. In Nigeria in the 1950's and 60's the writing of wills was considered unnecessary as people verbally instructed their families on what should happen after their death.

In Jemima's case my father's instructions were for his younger brother, Samuel, to marry her and inherit half his estate. In a bizarre twist it emerged that Jemima had previously been Samuel's girlfriend while they were at school together. However, Jemima had become pregnant and subsequently gave birth to a boy, Charles, who was exactly the same age as me. Charles was therefore born out of wedlock, which was not acceptable. The situation that had resulted was that Jemima required assistance with rehabilitation into the community and Samuel had helped by recommending her to my father as a suitable wife. The timing was good as 3 years had elapsed since my mother's death. Additionally, Jemima was extremely beautiful which made it hard for my father to resist. He fell in love with her, after a meeting arranged by Samuel, and they were married soon afterwards.

Four sons—Davidson, John, Joel, Godwin (who died young), and one daughter—Joel's twin, Juliet (who died about 6 months after birth) resulted from this marriage. These were my stepbrothers whom I had nursed as babies and we now all lived together on the farms around Nguru.

The work sequence took the form of obtaining a contract with a farmer to carry out weeding and planting. Payment started at £5 to complete the contracted work—this involved the entire family. Jemima was a hard taskmistress and drove me mercilessly. We would leave the compound early each day in order to take advantage of the morning cool, before the sun slowed us down after about 9am. We took mats, pots and pans to make a temporary camp which Jemima and I set up in the shade.

I was around 6 years old at this time, but my stepbrothers were all under 4 and too young to work. They were very restless and I was required to look after them as well as carrying out my labouring duties. This meant that, out of the six of us, only two could do the work. It was exhausting but in order to make a living we had to do this for 2 years, until my Uncle Samuel (Jemima's arranged husband) came back from Kano in Northern Nigeria, where he had set up a laundry business. He had lived in the North for many years and had a Muslim girlfriend (Funalny) by whom he had had 2 sons and one daughter. They had not married, as it was prohibited for Muslims to marry Christians, but somehow they managed to keep this a secret and his business had flourished. He was a very flamboyant and confident man and was able to handle the situation in his own way.

Now Samuel was able to devote attention to us and fulfil his brother's wishes. He was concerned with the welfare of his brother's children which was as much a duty for him as any love he may have felt for us. As a further precaution, the Muslim girlfriend was relocated to avoid any conflict in the new arrangement.

When Jemima told me that my Uncle Samuel was coming to take us all with him to Kano she added that, if I did not behave, she would leave me behind. I made a supreme effort to be accommodating in this respect since I sensed that the longed-for escape from the drudgery of farm work was at last becoming a reality.

What really concentrated my mind was that Samuel had said that he could only take 4 of us and that one child would have to be sent to Jemima's parents. This gave Jemima a threatening hold over me. However, what I didn't know was that Samuel had stipulated that I must be included in the move North since he had particularly promised my father that he would look after me. He would attempt to fulfill this promise whether he wanted to, or not.

To further complicate matters a telegram arrived telling us that Samuel could not come in person to collect us and that Jemima should make the travel arrangements for the four of us. He had sent money for this purpose. Jemima arranged for her eldest son, Davidson, to live with her parents in Amuzi. She then announced that we were to travel by train from Umuahia to Kano.

On the day of our departure most of the members of the Oparaji family gathered to wish us well and we were driven to Umuahia to catch the train. I was so excited as my life up to this point had been relentlessly tedious. I was eager for change yet I was still only 7 years old.

When we arrived at Kano railway station after 2 days of travel I spotted my Uncle Samuel in the crowd and I waved frantically to him through the carriage window. He walked alongside the train as it pulled into the platform and my feelings of love for him overwhelmed me. I couldn't wait to jump off as he opened the door. He hugged and kissed me and he called me 'Nne', which means mother, (a reference to my being the reincarnation of my grandmother and the only girl from my father's 9 children with Grace). Samuel eventually put me down to greet Jemima and I couldn't help but notice the dark expression on her face at being initially ignored. I recognised only too well this expression. She had a mental block where I was concerned and openly told Samuel that she was unhappy that he had greeted me before her.

This was the first of many arguments between them, most of which were because of me, and my feelings of rejection by others towards me were re-awakened, a reminder that I was a problem which emanated from the fact that I was an orphan with no direct link to an earthly parent. At this time Samuel was the closest I had to a substitute father and Jemima could not accept this so she made it her business to spoil my relationship with him. In fact, if she had shown the slightest warmth towards me it could have been so different and her affection would have been enough for me to feel some kind of human connection with her. Instead there was this constant competition between us which was based on jealousy and mistrust and I was intensely frustrated by the unfairness of this. As I was the minor I could only accept things as they developed. Looking back now it was an absurd situation but I was too young to make any sense out of it and, in order to compensate for this, my spirit hardened and my rebellious nature became more entrenched.

We proceeded from the station to Samuel's house at 11 Onacha Road. It was a comfortable two bedroom house in the Hausa style and the rooms had been well prepared for our arrival. I shared one room with my stepbrothers and now remember how uncontrollably happy I was at the sudden change in our lifestyle. However, I also have conflicting memories of this period which I can never shake off. The events which caused these later recollections were about to unfold.

Two days later an argument broke out between Samuel and Jemima over a bedwetting incident by me. This was a fundamental weakness of mine which I think was caused by a lack of potty training during the time I was growing up in the orphanage after the death of my mother. Incredibly children in hospitals and orphanages were not trained in the basic essentials and it had been left to me to develop these by instinct. Jemima had discovered the misdemeanour and started beating me with a shoe. Unlike my life in Ezuhu Nguru where I had silently borne my punishments I realised that my uncle could be used and, on this occasion, I started to scream hysterically to attract his attention. He came rushing in and shouted at Jemima to stop. He saw my face was swollen and bruised and took me to his shop next door where he consoled me.

Jemima, of course, was extremely angry at Samuel taking my side and told him that if this attitude persisted she would leave. Their relationship was unusual in that they were not married—in Igbo tradition a dead brother's wife is passed on to a male relative but this often does not result in marriage. Rather, it is more economical for an unmarried man to take over the widow of his brother than to waste a dowry on purchasing another wife, or even to go through a ceremony. This is built on the premise that once an Igbo woman has been purchased she is tied to her husband's family for life. Consequently, it was quite normal in those times for young widows to be passed on to bachelors in the same family.

In order to rescue the situation in which Samuel found himself, and to avoid the shame of Jemima leaving (which, if he'd thought about it, was extremely unlikely) he started supporting her in the conflict with me. He sometimes showed a softer side towards me when she was not around but the fondness between my uncle and me never fully returned. This contributed to my anti-social tendencies and I slid further into isolationism and bitterness.

I became morbid and started wishing I was dead, trying to work out ways of ending it all. Someone told me that smoking kills, and if you wanted to die that was the best way to do it, so I started by picking up dog ends from the ground. The first attempts made me cough and feel sick but I persevered until I could inhale without any detrimental effect. However, the reason for starting the habit wasn't manifesting itself so I decided to increase the treatment with the full thing. When I could, I bought packets of Camel or 3 Rings but still nothing happened. Worse, I was actually enjoying it and felt much calmer with my new found friend, nicotine. Of course I became, and still am, an addict and nothing anyone can say or do will dissuade me from the comfort I derive from the habit.

About a year later Jemima, who had been lifted from back breaking labour in the fields into a comfortable existence in a town house decided, out of boredom, to start trading by selling bread from a stall in front of the house. Samuel agreed to this in the way he was now agreeing to most things Jemima suggested, which disappointed me greatly. As I was now 10 I had eagerly been looking forward to attending school with my new friends in the area. However, Jemima had decided that I was required for her new business venture and, in any case, there was no vacancy at the school. Additionally I was told that there was no point in my going to school as I did not speak the Northern language (Hausa).

So I resigned myself to the inevitable and learned that the new routine required me to be up at 3am in order to be at the bakery at 5.30, queuing with other servants for the start of bread distribution. Jemima made it her business to wake me to ensure that I set off on time. On the return journey, carrying the bread on my head, I passed my friends on their way to school, smartly dressed in their new uniforms. I felt crushed.

For the first few days Jemima came with me to ensure that I knew what to do. Thereafter I was left to carry on by myself. On return from the bakery I would be given breakfast (bread and tea) and then sent to the city bus station 3 miles away with £15 worth of bread which I would sell from a stall. The remaining £10 of bread plus some vegetables were sold by Jemima from her stall in front of the house.

Despite not being at school I gradually became pleased at doing this work since it enabled me to escape the hostile atmosphere around my uncle's house. I mixed with local people, mostly servants, and started to

15

learn the Hausa language. In fact I now speak Hausa better than my native Igbo language. Sometimes, if I sold the bread before the end of the day, I stayed in the city begging for money rather than going home early. I became aware that I was pretty, and attractive to men who liked to touch me. They gave me 'dash' which greatly increased my earnings. I never gave the extra money to Jemima and used it instead to educate myself by paying 1 shilling for 2 hour classes with the Mallams, who taught reading and writing in Arabic and English at private schools in the city.

I began to regain some confidence in myself and found that by projecting my looks and character I could sell my bread quickly. This enabled me to get to my classes earlier and also buy my pencils and paper. No one at home knew anything about this; all they knew was that I left in the morning at 10am and returned at 5pm with the correct money. It was getting to the point where my first priority was my education and, if I didn't sell the bread by 2pm, I would cover it and go to my class. On these occasions I would return to the bus station after class and try to sell the rest of the bread. If I couldn't sell it I would take it home and tell Jemima it was unsold and give her the balance of the money. Luckily she didn't complain.

Jemima and my uncle never knew or even suspected what I was doing. My allowance from them was 1 shilling (5 new pence) for my lunch, but this was of secondary importance as I always had more money than they knew about. After about a year of bread trading I asked Uncle Samuel about my schooling. Probably feeling guilty about his promise to my father he agreed to investigate, but Jemima was not happy as it would mean a reduction in her business income. However, this time she was overruled and my uncle found me a vacancy in a local school. At last I was in uniform like the other children which was what I wanted more than anything.

I was now 9 and to my new teachers' surprise I was well ahead of my class and passing exams easily. My uncle had told them that I had just come from the East and might find it hard going. However, they told him that I was very advanced and intelligent. He was puzzled by this but, of course, he did not know that I had been secretly learning from the Mallams. In fact, by paying for my own lessons, I had been receiving vastly superior education than that available from the state system which I now attended.

Typically, Jemima decided that I should now start to sell bread after school to ensure that her income was not affected. School finished at 3pm therefore I had to be home at 3.30 to set off for the bus station. In addition I still had to collect the bread from the bakery in the morning as usual. So it was up at 3am to collect the bread at 5am, get home at 6am and set off for school at 7.30. I even sometimes managed to continue my private lessons with the Mallams, still giving priority to my lessons whether or not the bread was sold.

However this was a step too far. Things were getting complicated. On one occasion I sold my bread early and, exhausted, feel asleep at the bus station. I had tied the money into a cloth which I normally used to balance the bread on my head. When I awoke the money and the cloth were gone. I was distraught and no one I asked knew anything. I had lost £55 which was bad enough, but the reception I was going to get from Jemima was unthinkable. I cried and cried and begged at the bus station to try and make up the loss, and actually managed to make £32. Long after the other traders had gone I was still there begging. Some of the traders from the bus station were neighbours of my uncle and, on passing by his house, told Jemima about the money and that I was refusing to come home.

Adjacent to the bus station was a filling station run by a man called John. He noticed me sitting on my own, crying and begging, and asked others what was wrong. They told him the story and he came over to me to ask where I lived. He told me not to worry and gave me £23 to make up the loss, but I was still frantic and too frightened to go home as I knew I'd be punished severely whatever happened. However, John eventually persuaded me to leave and drove me home. He knocked at the door and my uncle opened the door.

"What do you want?" he demanded belligerently.

John explained what had happened and added that he had replaced the stolen money and everything was now ok. My uncle became abusive and told John that it was none of his business and to go away. In fact he started to accuse John of being involved in the loss of the money and threatened to take him to court for raping me. I felt awful that these 'true churchgoers' could stoop to such tactics and I promised myself that, if I ever grew up, I would not go to church because these people act like the devils they themselves denounce. At this, John could see that my fears were justified and told me that he would return the next day to make sure that I was alright. My uncle told him not to darken his door again so John gave up and left.

After John had gone I went apprehensively into the house and was immediately grabbed by my uncle. He tied my wrists and ankles with electric wire and proceeded to beat me with a koboka (leather braded strap) and put pepper in my eyes. My whole body was cut and bleeding from the punishment and when he had tired of this he stopped, and I crawled away into my room and hid under the bed, still tied up and semi-conscious.

I lay there all night and in the morning he came back and untied me. He was calmer and looked a bit sorry for what he had done, but Jemima, standing behind him, was jeering and looking extremely pleased at my state. I was very bruised and swollen with deep cuts all over my body, arms and legs. My eyes were painful and swollen from the pepper.

At this point, in my misery, I decided that I no longer wanted to live with my uncle and just lay on the floor too exhausted to move. My uncle seemed uncertain as to what to do since I was shaking uncontrollably, so he brought me some food. It was at this moment that I decided to run away as soon as possible.

After 2 days I felt able to go outside the front door. As I was sitting on the step John, from the filling station, suddenly arrived. He had been told by neighbours that they hadn't seen me since he'd brought me home so he'd come to see if I was alright. When he saw my cuts and bruises he called the police and told them that he'd given me the £23 to ensure that my uncle would not harm me. Now he wanted it back. Unfortunately, the police did very little apart from telling John and Samuel to sort it out themselves. But they did take me to the hospital

Later, Samuel and Jemima accused me of being used by men like John, otherwise, why would he have given me money? This strengthened my intention to run away from these 'Christians', especially as they now expected me to continue working, despite my injuries. I got together all the money I had accumulated, some of which I had hidden in the hollow bricks of the compound wall of my uncle's house. Together with the money collected while begging, and that given to me to buy bread that morning, I had a total of £78.

I went to a kinsman from my village, called Lawrence, who lived 2 miles away and told him my story. He allowed me to stay with him for a week to get better. Then he decided to go to Samuel to ask why he had treated me in this way. I agreed to go with him but only to get the address of my eldest brother, Ambrose, who was a soldier in the Nigerian army. He lived in Zaria and I thought that, if I could find him, I would ask if I could live with him for a while. In fact Lawrence went by himself to get Ambrose's address by subterfuge, which he managed to do. He brought the address to me and we went back together to my uncle's house. After a heated discussion I told Samuel and Jemima that I would kill myself if I had to return to their house or, alternatively, run away.

In fact I made up my mind to run away immediately and bought some decent second hand clothes with the bread money. I didn't want my brother to see me in my old bloodstained garments. Lawrence contacted my brother, Ambrose, to tell him what had happened to me and he said he would come over to Lawrence's house, where I was living. Then we would all drive to my uncle's house to confront him over what he had done to me. When he saw me my brother was shocked and immediately said that I should go and live with him. He told Samuel that I was leaving and would not be returning.

I remember feeling disappointed that my schooling would now be disrupted, but I had to get away from these evil relatives.

CHAPTER 3

Gathering Storm Clouds

Thus began a very pleasant period of my life. Ambrose treated me like a queen and made me feel wanted and proud. At last a member of the Opariji family had made me feel that life was worth living after all. He was a handsome bachelor and very popular with his friends whom I got to know very well. I don't think I would have had it better anywhere else.

He even sent me to the best school, paid for my hair to be done and provided me with a driver who had instructions to take me anywhere I wanted. From habit I felt compelled to carry on doing the housework, but soon realised that servants in the house were being paid to do this. My new life took a lot of getting used to. I found that I could get on very well with new acquaintances but that I couldn't seem to relate to family members. I couldn't explain this and still wonder why this phenomenon existed. There were so many 'evil' people in my extended family.

Anyway, I didn't care, Ambrose had brought joy into my life, and I really mean unforgettable joy. The drudgery of getting up early to queue for bread, the abuse and beatings for no good reason, were only distant memories and I was able to to mix and play with other children for the first time in my life. My brother cared for me and everything was wonderful. I wished it could go on forever.

For 2 years everything was perfect until, in the middle of 1966, Ambrose became worried that the political tensions in the North might make things difficult for Easteners living there. Therefore, he arranged for me to be driven home to my compound in Nguru, Mbaise. To my surprise, on my arrival, I found Uncle Samuel, Jemima and my stepbrothers already living there. They had escaped from Kano at the same time that I had left

Zaria and, once again, I found myself living with them. The clock had been turned back and I felt very depressed at this turn of events.

The situation in the North was becoming very serious for the Igbos but Ambrose thought he was safe for the time being, as he was a soldier in the Nigerian army. It was the Igbo civilians who were being targeted and many were killed in the riots before they could flee. So he continued to live in his house after I had left. He had given me about £1000 to take with me, which was very far sighted of him as we were to discover later.

During my time living with Ambrose I had blossomed and had become much more astute. He had given me pocket money to spend on myself and I had beautiful clothes. Additionally he had given me the £1000 to look after, if things in the North deteriorated. Now the family was together again, in the Oparaji compound, but under different circumstances. I felt much more in control of my relationship with Jemima,

The compound was very large and in traditional Igbo style. It consisted of about 11 houses (each with two or three rooms) within a perimeter wall. It accommodated about 120 people in total. Grandparents, fathers, mothers, their children and their childrens' children all lived in the compound. Each son (Mbaise daughters were irrelevant and only useful for marrying off and obtaining dowries) had his own house containing his family which grew as he married and had children. Outside the compounds the lower status villagers (our kinsmen) lived in smaller dwellings.

So here I was again. The difference was that I was no longer treated as a child slave because I had money, had learnt self-respect, and was much more capable at dealing with my elders. Jemima was very nice to me and it was obvious why. She was only interested in the money she knew I had, and often asked me about it. Of course I had hidden it and told her nothing, but every so often I would produce just enough to enable her to feed us all, thus keeping her where I could control the situation. She knew how well I had been living since we parted after the beating I had taken at the hands of Samuel.

Ambrose had once taken me back to visit Samuel and Jemima when I lived with him in Kano. I had taken £60 with me which I had saved from my pocket money. I chose a moment to casually give Jemima £10, which had astonished her. But she quickly recovered and, guessing that I had more, offered to look after it for me, but I wasn't as stupid as she thought and gave her no more. During that visit I also gave Samuel £50 which shocked him also. I purposely did this to make them feel uncomfortable for their treatment of me. But I don't suppose they thought of it that way, they were too self-centred for that kind of sentiment.

However, as I grew older I began to grudgingly appreciate the way I was brought up. It was about this time that I adopted my motto for life—'Everything happens for a purpose'. It prepared me very well for the horrific times which were coming. When Nigeria and Biafra fought a civil war I stood for myself throughout and fought alongside the men. One thing for which my harsh upbringing prepared me was the ability to mentally absorb punishment, face difficult situations, and come back stronger than before. I also cannot bear a grudge for long and almost always forgive my transgressors. Another side of me is that I want to help people so much, even to the extent of going short myself. It is a failing of mine, but I think it is a good failing.

I lived in one of the compound houses with Uncle Samuel, Jemima, and her 4 children. Life became dull again. Samuel was getting old and was depressed at having lost the lifestyle he had enjoyed in the North. What money he had been able to bring from Kano was running out and there was no work available in the village, other than the awful farm labouring. Jemima was tormented by the knowledge that I still had money and continually tried to find out how much there was. I used to amuse myself by wondering what she would have done if she had known that I had £800.

I had wrapped the money in a cloth which I hid in the thatched eaves of my house. Every morning I checked that it was safe but, to my horror, one morning it was not there. I panicked thinking that Jemima had discovered it and, with a pounding heart, turned to start walking back through the compound, wondering what to do. Suddenly I saw the cloth bundle lying on the ground. I quickly grabbed it and, looking around to make sure no one had seen me, feverishly unwound the cloth to see if the money was still there. It was, and I felt the dizzy rush of relief. I could only assume an animal, maybe a rat, had disturbed the bundle and immediately started to think of a safer hiding place

I finally decided to bury it in the ground in a quiet corner of the compound. I dug a hole with a knife, wrapped the money in a cellophane bag and stuffed it into an old Carnation milk tin in order to protect it from the damp and insects. I had to be careful that no one saw me doing this and I was scared of visiting it in case I was seen. In fact I was so fearful of being discovered at the hiding place that I didn't go there at all. Anyway, I was self-sufficient without the bulk of the money and had about £5 and all my toiletries—cream, soap and clothing brought from the North, and didn't need to go to the market for anything. I even gave some of my friends pomade (skin cream) and soap, and to Jemima I gave £2-10s (£2.50p) on two occasions. I then told her the money had run out.

From that moment my usefulness to Jemima and Samuel ceased and my rations became smaller and smaller so I started to help other women in the compound by looking after their children to get extra food. My stepmother took exception to this and argued with the women, complaining that I was being distracted away from my work for her. But I had a healthy appetite and needed more food than I was being given by her, so I continued to do this. I felt absolutely no loyalty whatsoever towards Jemima and Samuel following their disregard and cruelty towards me.

During this time I never went back to the buried money and, in any case, I had always assumed that my brother, Ambrose, had originally given it to me to look after until I saw him again. It wasn't mine. On the day I left his house he had said that he would probably join us if the situation in the North deteriorated so I was keeping it for him, thinking that he wouldn't mind if I used small amounts for my upkeep.

So life in the Oparaji family compound continued without much excitement. We heard reports of the disturbances and conflict between our people and the Hausas in the North, but it didn't affect us in Mbaise. I often thought of Ambrose, nostalgically recalling how idyllic my life had been with him during those 2 short years.

One evening in late 1966 we were sitting around the communal fireplace with the older people discussing the crisis in the North. I heard them say that another train had arrived at the town station full of dead and dying Igbo people suffering from hideous wounds. They said that the atrocities that had been carried out on these people were horrific. For example, one practice was the forcing of a stick into the rectums of victims before throwing them on to trains bound for the East. Many of the corpses and those dying had this injury when the train arrived. It was assumed that this was to serve as a warning that Easterners were no longer welcome in the North. The people of the towns in the East were becoming fearful for the safety of their relatives who were in the North, but had not yet returned. I again thought of Ambrose and wondered if I would ever see him again.

However, on another evening in early 1967, after eating, the families had gathered as usual in the central house (Ovu) where the elders were telling the younger ones stories past and present. Suddenly, a figure appeared out of the darkness dressed only in underpants. I was astonished and overwhelmed to see that it was Ambrose and rushed to embrace him. I had given up hoping that I would ever see him again but here he was, albeit looking incongruous but, sure enough, it was my dear brother. My stepmother ran into the house to get a wrapper for him and I continued to hug him while he continually told me that he was sure it was the thought of me that had kept him alive. He was so happy to be home, surrounded by friendly people, and so relieved to be able to live to tell the tale.

After he had eaten and felt comfortable we settled down to hear his story. He had decided to desert from the army and escape as the rioting and antagonism towards the Igbo, even those serving in the army, was getting worse. He had hit on the idea of removing most of his clothes to feign madness in order to avoid the attention of the Hausas and managed to get to the station. Like many others he had left with only what he had on his person, but felt lucky to be able to keep his life. It had been his final chance to escape as he had heard on the radio that this was the last train to the East. When he had boarded the train dressed only in his pants, but uninjured, he found he was surrounded by dead and half dead fellow countrymen. So he pretended to be ill to avoid attention. On arrival at Omuahia station (the terminal for trains from the North) he was able to walk to Ezuhu Nguru, a distance of 28 miles.

Word of his arrival spread and many people came to our compound to try and get news of other missing relatives and friends in the North. Unfortunately, he couldn't do much to help them due to the chaotic situation from which he had escaped. He told them that it was each person for himself and that people were disappearing daily without trace.

The day after he arrived I privately approached Ambrose to tell him that I had good news for him. I told him about the money which I had assumed he'd given me for safe keeping. He then said he'd given it to me for my personal use and was astonished to hear that some of the £1000 remained. He asked me who was looking after it and I told him that I couldn't trust anybody and had buried it. He looked at me with incredulity and asked where it was hidden. I said that we couldn't touch it yet as my stepmother was under the impression that I was penniless. We would have to wait until no one was around before digging it up.

Two days later everyone was out of the compound and I told Ambrose that now was the time to retrieve it. I showed him the spot then Ambrose got a hoe and, with one chop, hit the tin. Obviously I hadn't buried it very deeply. He cleaned the mud off the cloth, unwrapped the tin and counted the money. He was clearly overcome at how much was left after 6 months, hugged me and repeatedly called me 'Nne' (mother). He was so happy to find that he had not lost everything after all.

Ambrose took £100 and went to Owerri to buy clothes and necessities. While shopping he heard about the existence, nearby, of barracks for the new Biafran army which was being formed following the decision to secede from Nigeria after a failed peace summit in Ghana. Ambrose went to the army camp to make enquiries about enlisting and was accepted immediately. He came back and told me that he would be moving on and I felt a mixture of disappointment and happiness at the way things had turned out. He took £200 leaving me with the balance which he said I should hide in a hollow bed leg. This would be safer than burying it.

In the months following my beloved brother's departure from the compound, after such a short stay, life continued monotonously for the rest of us. We tried to make a living as before on the farms since this was really the only option for scratching a living. Ambrose had told me that he would initially be serving close to home and would be able to visit us as often as possible. As the months passed and the conflict between the Biafrans and the Nigerian Government forces intensified we started to find moving around and holding on to any kind of work almost impossible. Air raids made life riskier and, as houses were mostly made of aluminum, they made an easy target for the Nigerian Air Force.

We decided to move out of the permanent houses during the day to try and carry on with the farm work. We felt safer in the country. The sounds of aircraft, gunfire and explosions were constant and life became intolerable due to the scarcity of food, salt, etc., combined with the uncertainty of how long the war would last. What we did know was that the fighting was getting closer to Mbaise. I never saw Ambrose again, despite his promise to keep in touch with us. Likewise, my other brothers, who had joined the Biafran army before him, never returned to the village. However, I was never really close to my brothers (it was only by chance that I had got to know Ambrose so well) as I was much younger than them and my life had existed in a different atmosphere, with guardians and a stepmother to bring me up.

We were constantly hungry and I had to resort to using the hidden money more and more. Jemima was finding it difficult to cope with the shortages so I secretly used the money to buy food for us and pretended to her that it had been given to me by people I met. In typical fashion she saw the worst in this and accused me of, 'messing about with men', to obtain the food. Of course I didn't tell her the truth about the money and, eventually, it ran out anyway. She didn't complain about the food I brought back but still accused me of being loose, which was very unfair on a twelve year old girl.

CHAPTER 4

A Change of Life

In 1967 one of my uncles, Festus, came to visit us from his station where he was the headmaster of a primary school at Lorge, about 14 miles from Ezuhu Nguru. He saw that I was in constant conflict with my stepmother and decided to take me into his household, to work as a servant and continue with my schooling. There were three other children (all cousins of mine) doing the same thing—and used as servants in his house when we weren't studying. He was affectionally known to us as 'Brother Festus' and as a strict, but good man, doing his duty by helping his less fortunate relatives. I was the oldest of this group of children and this gave me the chance to complete Standard 6 which, in Nigeria at that time, was tied to the British education system. I became excited at the prospect of continuing my education which, to me, was the most important factor in my life.

I became the mother to the other servants and organised the housework, cooking, and making sure they attended their classes, in addition to arranging rotas for such activities as bringing water from the stream, 3 miles away. My uncle's routine was very demanding and there was no room for any slack. I did my best but the other children (3 boys; Claytus (8), Kenneth (7), and George (4)) were not perfect, and when things were omitted or not performed correctly we were all punished severely. This normally took the form of a whipping with a cane from a selection that Brother Festus kept for this purpose. He accepted no excuses but, as this was normal discipline in Africa, we accepted our lot uncomplainingly since we knew that he had extended a lifeline to us for which we were incredibly grateful.

However, on one occasion Festus went too far. Claytus had sneaked off to play football instead of doing his work, thinking that his uncle had gone away for the day. Unfortunately, Festus returned unexpectedly and, after parking his bicycle, noticed that Claytus was absent. He was furious and his temper had built up to boiling point by the time Claytus turned up. Festus had his cane ready and, grabbing the terrified boy, started a whipping which was so severe that Claytus broke free and took off, running through the house and into the kitchen where I was doing the cooking. As he came through the door he barged into me, nearly pushing me into the fire. I was seized with anger at this and decided, there and then, that enough was enough. Grabbing my large pestle I launched myself towards Festus as he followed in hot pursuit of his victim. I blocked his way and shouted at him,

"This is madness, do you want to kill us all?"

As I had prevented Festus from continuing with the chase he turned on me, blindly striking out with his cane. I stood my ground and, waving my pestle in his face, yelled, "Stop it! I've had enough of this."

He stood there for a moment, a shocked expression replacing the anger on his face. He'd never seen me in this mood and, without a word, turned and left the kitchen.

Brother Festus reading the lesson in the church,
re-built by me after I had burnt it down.

28

This was a turning point and I was never whipped by him again. He was now unsure of what he might unleash, as far as I was concerned, and I was determined to use this victory to good effect. The following week Brother Festus went home to Ezuhu Nguru for the weekend so I decided to take the opportunity to put an end to his brand of punishment. I went into his room and, gathering up all his canes, took them outside and broke them up for use as firewood. When he returned there was no reaction from him until, one day, one of my cousins stepped out of line. Festus came to me in an agitated state demanding to know where his canes had gone. I told him what I had done, pointing out that I could have been badly burnt due to his nonsense with Claytus. His response to this was predictable.

"Well, you're now going to have to replace them yourself, aren't you?" he said, smiling triumphantly.

I didn't smile, responding as confidently as I could with, "I'm not going to have anything to do with any canes, and if you don't like it I'm leaving your house and going home."

This was a dangerous moment for me as my continued education was now in the balance. But Festus didn't pursue his point, and I didn't have to leave. However, his brand of punishment did continue, but much less frequently and he virtually ignored me from then on.

I was now starting to experience the effects of hormonal change. I think this was partly triggered by the fact that I had been pushed to take Standard 6 exams even though I was in the Standard 5 age bracket. If I didn't do this I would be qualified as Elementary in the Nigerian system. The colonial education structure was in the final stages of being phased out following Independence and the Nigerian system was being installed. I subsequently passed Standard 6 with distinction. However, this was not appreciated by my extended family of Uncles, Aunties, etc., which made me feel bitter since many of them had been helped by my father. Once again the familiar feelings of rejection and isolation returned and I had to resort to thinking and acting for myself.

Festus considered that, having passed my grades, his commitment to me had been fulfilled. He explained that it was time for me to return to our compound. He was glad to see me go since my resistance to his methods of discipline was affecting his authority with the others. He suggested that other relatives (some of whom had been helped by my father) should now contribute to my secondary education. I did try contacting some of them but this was mostly met with disinterest. They all had their own problems to deal with and the war was causing people to lose interest in good causes.

I, therefore, returned to live with my stepmother and spent my time roaming about the village when I wasn't doing jobs for her. My friends in Mbaise were all moving on with their education and my bitterness and frustration grew. Without parents I was either ignored or, at best, treated with indifference by most of the families in our compound. My proud spirit could not cope with this. Then I met an old friend, Virginia, back from her schooling for the holidays and she decided we should visit a man friend who had asked her to come and see him at his home.

Virginia's friend, Alex, was a divisional officer in Aboh local government. Virginia wanted support and asked me to come along. However, the situation changed when we arrived. His attention immediately focused on me and he appeared very impressed with my dancing. We spent the afternoon chatting pleasantly during which he asked me which school I attended. I managed to evade that question. Then he offered to drop us off at our homes when it was time to leave. He wanted to let Virginia off first but she insisted that I was taken home first, which he did. But he came straight back to my house after leaving Virginia and asked me if he could meet my parents. I told him that I lived with my stepmother which didn't seem to put him off. So I reluctantly went to tell Jemima that someone wanted to see her. On meeting him, she openly gave Alex the impression that she was astonished that a responsible man with a car should be interested in someone like me. She actually told him that I was stubborn and vindictive and wasn't worth bothering about. This didn't deter him and he took me back to his house after asking Jemima's permission, which she gave without hesitation. She really didn't care about me and thought I was a lost cause anyway.

I was fascinated with Alex, his house and music collection. He was also very handsome and much older than me, 30 to my 13. In fact I adored everything about him and was convinced that I was in love. At one point he said that he would like to marry me, but I told him that I would not be interested in marriage until I finished my education, which was the most important thing to me. I told him that my father had lived in Ireland for many years after he had come back from the fighting in World War II and used to tell me that he would send me to Ireland as soon I was 10 years old. I said that he died before that ambition was fulfilled but I still dreamt of it. Alex said he was sorry and would see me through university before thinking of marriage. I became excited at this and told him my choice of school would be Owerri Girls College, but he suggested that I should go to Mbaise Girls School as it was closer to his house.

We spent the night together—I danced for him, and with him, and felt for the first time in my life the magic of a loving relationship with someone outside the Oparaji circle. My current existence had left me wide open to this unbelievable situation, and I can truly say I was completely immersed in it and would have done anything for him. We slept together but he was very respectful and nothing more than a bit of fun occurred.

Three days later I enrolled at the college and suddenly I was on track again. Alex bought me a Honda Moblet (scooter) and now I was every inch the young lady zipping about town, totally transformed from the dejected character of only a week before.

Then, as so often happened in my roller coaster life, everything changed. The war was now dominating everyone's life and Alex received his call-up notice to join the new Biafran army. He was not pleased but had to obey and proceeded to make arrangements for my care during his absence. I was given an allotment of £7 per month which was to be paid by his younger brother Dr Aka who worked in Aboh General Hospital. This brother was not subject to call-up due to his job and I saw him at his office every month to collect my allowance.

On one occasion while I was in his office he invited me to lunch at his residence. I accepted, not suspecting the brother of my fiancé of any devious intentions, and we had a pleasant meal combined with polite conversation. We talked about the war and I was keen to know how Alex was faring not having seen or spoken to him for some time. After lunch we talked about my health, which I thought was a bit odd, and he produced some pills which he said would be good for me. He took a couple himself to put me at ease and, not suspecting anything, I took two of the pills and that was the last thing I remembered. I awoke in darkness, lying on a bed or couch, and feeling pain between my legs. I called out and the doctor came into the room, putting the light on and saying how sorry he was. I then noticed blood on the bed and felt ill.

He looked agitated and said, "Don't worry it'll heal and Alex will not know anything if you don't mess around with other men. Please don't tell him anything about this."

I didn't reply and asked him to get me out of his house. I was panic stricken and just wanted to get out of there and away from him as fast as possible. He took me to the door and I stumbled out, limping home through the night, sobbing.

After a few days of thinking about this incident I became extremely angry, and told a friend, Eugenie, who suggested that we should get some boys to beat up the doctor, but in the end I did nothing. It was another step on the learning curve.

Three months after that incident Alex returned from the frontline with a bullet wound in his back. He was admitted to Aboh Hospital, where his brother worked, and I visited him. He immediately remarked that I looked different which made me nervous. He commented on this saying that I wasn't the Irene he remembered. I was uncomfortable with this development and could not help thinking that he knew something had happened. This made me more uneasy and, in turn, probably increased any suspicions he may have had.

I tried to carry on as normal and visited him every day, but he continued to comment on my demeanour. He was eventually discharged as an outpatient two weeks later and returned to his house where I was supposed to be living. Actually I had moved out of his house, as it was too big for me on my own, and had gone back to my compound. I now had to move back in with Alex and was dreading the thought of what would happen if, and when, he discovered the truth.

On the first night that we were together in his house we sat down to dinner. I was relieved that he was acting more normally now. He started discussing how we would travel to London after the war so I could continue with my studies there. But, he said, we must first cement the relationship. He remarked that he could have been killed during the fighting and I would never have seen him again. He explained that, as he was due to return to the front, he wanted to make sure that we were truly man and wife and, if a child resulted, then I would have someone to remember him by, should the worst happen.

I began to feel uncomfortable again since he seemed to be acting as though he knew something was wrong but couldn't exactly identify what it was. He had not penetrated me before he'd gone away telling me that if he had opened the door others might have walked in. So, he said, tonight was the time for the long wait to end. But first we must enjoy our dinner. It was an excruciatingly painful hour or so for me. I had to endure the meal without an appetite, while at the same time anticipating the awful prospect of what might happen when the discovery was made.

At last dinner was over and we went to his room where we undressed and lay down together. He was older than me and very experienced, whereas I was only 13 which was the age at which many African girls were taken as wives. I was very scared since, despite my innocence, I knew that the awful moment had arrived. Alex had skilfully employed his foreplay and I did my best to respond. After a short time he moved to the entry position and I felt him force his way in. There was a pause, then silence suddenly broken by an explosion, not of passion, but rage. He withdrew immediately, pulled me off the bed and told me to stand up; then kneel down in front of him. He was shouting, incoherently, about killing me and dumping my body in the forest where it would never be found, unless I told him the truth about who had cheated on him and how it had happened.

I was petrified and unable to speak while he went to another room before returning with an army web belt. He whacked me full strength with the belt several times, pausing at intervals to shout at me, demanding to know how and why I had done this to him. I tried to answer, babbling anything I could think of, but whatever I said had no effect on him and he continued to rain down blows on all areas of my head, arms, legs and body. I was convinced that he was going to kill me, so I eventually blurted out the involvement of his brother. He kept on beating me and I became more desperate to get the facts out in the hope he would stop.

Eventually, through his rage, he began to comprehend what I was saying and stopped. He had probably exhausted himself more than anything. I was numb with pain and trauma and lay in a heap on the floor unable to think clearly. I think I was only semi-conscious.

Then he began to speak—demanding to know if I had told anyone else about my 'crime'. I said that only my friend Eugenie knew. This only enraged him again and he resumed the beatings with greater intensity. I felt like giving up and accepting the inevitable when he suddenly stopped and left the room. This gave me the chance to try and escape and, knowing the house well, I ran to the back door, managed to open it and staggered out into the open. I ran to Virginia's house, which was nearby, and banged on her door until her mother opened it to find me wrapped in a sheet, half collapsed and covered in blood. She called Virginia to come quickly and between them they half carried me to the hospital where I was suddenly struck dumb. I was unable to speak a word so no one knew what had happened to me.

I was put in a ward on my own and Virginia stayed the night with me. Next morning the doctors came in and examined me—I was still unable to tell them anything so Virginia had to make up a story to try and account for my condition. My injuries included deep cuts from the brass buckles on the belt and, as I had been naked at the time, these were all over my body, especially my arms, where I had tried to protect myself. The doctors had to treat me on the basis of what they could see and feel as I was still dumbstruck with shock. In actual fact my speechless state was partly due to the fact that my story would implicate the hospital and Alex's brother with all the follow-on effects that would result. I couldn't cope mentally with the added complications of this. However, what I didn't know, as I lay in my hospital bed, was that Alex had confronted his brother, Dr. Aka, with the facts and had threatened to kill him. The doctor took the easy route by deciding to disappear and I never saw him again.

I was visited once by my stepmother who in her waspish way told me that I had finally been caught out and had deserved all that I got. She honestly thought I was a loose girl and beyond redemption. She never came to visit me again in the hospital, and never sent any food, which is necessary to supplement the meagre hospital rations. My constant visitor was Virginia who came daily with food prepared by her mother, although I could not eat comfortably due to an injury to my mouth. On one visit she told me she had encountered Alex in the town and had told him that I was still in hospital. This was about 4 days after the attack and Virginia said that he had been surprised to hear I was in hospital at all. One day he appeared beside my bed and I panicked and started to scream, which brought nurses rushing in to the ward. I was still screaming when they came in and Alex was standing there, repeating self-consciously, "I'm sorry, I'm sorry, I'm sorry."

As I would not quieten down the nurses suggested that Alex should leave and he was ushered out of the room. Two days later he walked back in and I again started to break down. He looked startled, threw an envelope on the bed, and fled. After some deliberation I opened the envelope and found it contained £300 and a note saying that I should look after myself and forget all about him.

After leaving hospital I returned to the family compound where Jemima resumed her gloating and persecution of me. My misfortune at the hands of Alex had strengthened her belief that I was a hopeless case and had only got what I deserved. She mercilessly criticised me over my every action, in addition to making sure that the other aunties were aware that I was no good. I was expected to work only for Jemima but, in order to eat sufficiently, I had to work for other members of the Oparaji family in the compound. But Jemima did not accept this and continued to make trouble for me. All I had to supplement my miserable existence was the money that Alex had unceremoniously dumped on my hospital bed. However, I was careful not to spend that unnecessarily.

Eventually I got so fed up that I started to behave badly and, one day after an argument, left the compound to go to the next village where I met some people of my own age group who asked me to go to a party that evening. I decided that I would stay the night there as I was not wanted in my own compound. However, this turned out to one of the worst nights of my life.

I was very happy during the party and danced with many of the boys who were much older than me. One of these boys took an interest in me and, as I was on my own without a friend or family member, kept coming over to me, but I showed no interest in him and spent the evening avoiding him. I wasn't too worried as his friends were there and I felt no danger in the situation, eventually falling asleep in a chair at the end of the party. I suddenly woke up to find that four of these boys had grabbed me and were carrying me outside the compound. They ripped my clothes and started interfering with me. I couldn't escape and one after another they satisfied themselves. I was crying hysterically but they smothered my mouth and, as much as I struggled, I couldn't get away. They were too strong, so believing I was going to die, I fell back and pretended to be dead.

I heard them talking amongst themselves, saying that I might be dead and working out what they should do next. Eventually I heard them decide to carry me further away from their compound and dump me in the bush, which is what they did. I lay there for some time until I was sure that there was no one around, got up and, despite the agony of my injuries, managed to walk to Virginia's house, arriving as it was getting light. Virginia and her mother opened the door to let me in and I told them my story. Virginia was horrified, especially as this was the second similar incident in a short space of time, and asked why I hadn't invited her to go with me to the party. I told her that I had spontaneously walked out of my compound after an argument with my stepmother and had stopped at the first village I came to. Anyway I knew that Virginia's mother would not let her out at night.

With my best friend Virginia (left) who was there for me
with her family when I was alone and hungry.

I stayed with Virginia and her mother for about a week while I recovered from the shock and injuries sustained in the attack. I then reluctantly went back to my compound and Jemima, since there was nowhere else to go. I eventually decided that I could not stay there and made up my mind to go and look for Alex. After all he had shown some remorse by leaving me money and, with the people I had around me, he was probably my best option in the circumstances. Anyway, I was worn out by the constant objectionable attitude of Jemima and most of the people in the compound towards me. My mind was becoming hardened against them and I just wanted to be rid of the daily conflicts.

Also I had no one else in my life and Alex's money had almost gone. I had been told that he was the adjutant of an army camp at Irualla which was some distance from my home. So I set out with my few possessions to hitchhike there. In fact I walked the whole way as I never got a lift. It took 3 days and I slept rough in market squares at night. Luckily it was fairly safe to travel in this area as the war had not yet reached this part of Biafra.

As I got closer to the camp I asked people if they knew Alex and described him. Eventually a soldier was able to help me and directed me to an impressive looking house. I knocked on the door and a servant let me in, remarking that I looked like the captain's wife. I didn't understand why he had said this until I saw Alex's room which was covered in photographs he had taken of me when we were together.

Alex had a girlfriend, a local girl, and they were out walking when I arrived. This gave me the opportunity to clean up and make myself more presentable. I smelled so much that I couldn't stand it myself. When they returned I suddenly felt worried that he might attack me again. However, he appeared overjoyed to see me and embraced me tightly. He then informed his girlfriend, who was standing nearby looking upset, that she would have to leave as his fiancé had returned. She collected her belongings and Alex arranged for a vehicle and driver to take her home.

We had an enjoyable evening together and it was an immense relief for me as I had expected a different kind of reaction from him. I enjoyed being with him as he really was a very considerate man when he wanted to be. However, my own character was developing fast and my main aim was now self preservation. If that meant using people then so be it. I would only give men favours if it suited me and made me happy. Anyway, Alex was already flawed in my mind since he had shown me what he was capable of, and, whether I liked it or not, I had to be on my guard. I would stay with him for as long as it suited me.

CHAPTER 5

Anger and Flames

I lived with Alex in his house for about 4 months and during that time he was convinced that we were going to get married. His thoughts constantly revolved around our marriage plans and he endlessly discussed the involvement of our respective families. What he couldn't comprehend was that I had no intention of marrying him. I was still only 13 and had only one ambition which was to further my education. He had promised, when we first met, that I would accompany him to London where he was due to study at University, but this had been postponed by the war so my personal plans had to be revised to take account of the new situation.

Alex was desperate for a child and, each month, when my period arrived he became angry. Gradually the monster in him re-emerged and the beatings started. My feelings hardened against him once more, although I had prepared myself for this. After a beating I would look at him while he slept and often felt the urge to finish him off there and then. I assumed that he could sleep peacefully since, by my coming to find him after his first attack on me, I had shown him that I had accepted his dominance as a dutiful wife should. Luckily for us both I never put my urges into practice.

I therefore manipulated the situation to my own advantage since I did not want a child, nor did I want to get married so young. Alex was very capable at looking after me but I was not interested in him or his desires, only in what he could do for me. There were many things I did not like about marriage having observed the habits of many couples. For instance in those days my tribe, the Igbo, had bad customs where women were concerned. They didn't believe in training girls to a high standard of education, they always said that a woman's place is in the kitchen.

The father of a baby girl only thinks of the dowry he can get as soon as she is 15, or even less. So as soon as a girl is at the right age she is ready to be married off, unless she is lucky enough to come from a very rich family. In that case it is alright to stay with her parents if she is interested in education. If she is intelligent then some encouragement will be given to her and she may get into university. This means that only rich men can try to marry her. But the average man will not dare to try and get near her as he would be made aware that, since so much money had already been spent on her, he would have to very self-sufficient. He would also be expected to be qualified to at least the same level as his wife.

In my case my family wasn't interested in my education. They hoped that a rich man would come forward and marry me for my bodily attractions and housekeeping skills and, of course, the dowry that I might get them. However, with the half education I had got for myself and from Alex, and, with the beauty people said I had, I decided to oppose the tradition and to continue to further myself in my own way. My strategy for this was to convince everyone I was bad which, hopefully, would deter my family and rich men alike.

I loved dancing and going to parties which was not right in the eyes of the traditionalists. So they saw no future in me and no hope of getting a dowry. I had no parents to claim the dowry, but that didn't matter as my blood relatives would have a share in it, if they could. But I wasn't going to give them that satisfaction. Most of them were people I would not like to help so I made sure they saw only the bad side of me. Therefore, I was of no use to any of them so they either ignored or disliked me. This suited me and was the way I was going to move on from this point. After all they had labelled me as a Spiritual Child (Witch) so what was the point of fighting it?

In the meantime Alex's frustration and anger grew in intensity and I realised that I had better move sooner rather than later. His plans for our wedding were developing fast. He had arranged for some members of his family to visit mine in order to make plans for the traditional engagement. I therefore made the decision to leave him immediately and one morning, after he had gone to work, I left, leaving all my belongings behind to buy time and get some distance between us before he realised what had happened. I walked out and, with some money that I had saved, went to a close friend, Regina Igwe, who lived in Arondisuogo, about 20 miles from the army camp. I didn't want to go back to my home as that was the first place Alex would look.

Regina and her mother, whose husband had been a police sergeant in Mbaise but had died there, welcomed me to their home where I spent the next few months. We (Regina and I) spent our time roaming the countryside around Arondisuogo and Mbaise begging for food, mostly at the Catholic Reverend Fathers' houses where the war relief supplies were stored. The war had not yet affected this area so we could travel in reasonable safety. The Catholic priests got their pleasures from young girls like us in return for some of the food donated by countries sympathetic to Biafra, which they were supposed to distribute free to their parishes. The children, who knew what they were doing, begged at these church residencies and, if they were 'lucky/attractive', were invited in.

We lived well using this system. The procedure was for us to be locked in a room so the servants didn't see us before they went off duty. We were kept in the house until late at night and then, when the Reverend Fathers had satisfied themselves, we were taken out and dropped off where we could get transport back to Regina's house. On the journey home we would sell some of the food to people for cash and keep the rest to give to Regina's mother for her other children. Public transport was extremely scarce and most motor travel was accomplished by hitching. The most reliable form of travel was that made on foot—I must have walked hundreds, if not thousands of miles during the war.

I periodically returned to my compound to take food and money to Jemima for my stepbrothers. Once Jemima remarked that, as I was getting older, I should think about confirmation and all my friends were preparing for this. I agreed because I come from a very religious family and felt close to my Protestant faith, despite my experiences of 'Christians'. My paternal grandfather was actually involved in helping the missionaries establish the Protestant church in the area around his village, Ezuhu Nguru.

Every Christian child was expected to go to church and behave responsibly, (i.e. obey their elders and not misbehave). However, I was a special case being an orphan. I was considered a 'labelled child' since my mother had died at my birth and for this reason I was automatically branded as bad or evil—traditionally a witch, and every woman was entitled to be offensive towards me. I was used by all the female members of the Oparaji family since I was 'spare' (i.e. not owned by a natural mother). They all had a claim on me for work purposes in return for feeding me. There was no love involved in their treatment of me.

My family's faith had become complicated when my father's elder brother, Aloyisus, married Lucy who was a Catholic. He then adopted her faith. I know this because I had asked my grandfather why there was some of each faith in the Oparaji family. He was not worried by the mixture of faiths and, in any case Aloyisus loved Lucy very much. However, I remember Lucy as a vindictive and cruel women but that was probably because of the tendency of the women to treat me according to my status. She would have been no worse than the others in the compound.

My grandfather told me that the first white missionary was killed and hung from a large tree in the village of Ahariah. We all knew this tree and it was well known as the hanging place of the first missionary. I don't know whether he was Protestant or Catholic but one thing is certain the Nigerian people in this area were, at first, angry at being told to disown their pagan gods and embrace Christianity. The tree is actually now in a Catholic Church compound.

Some people threw their idols away or burnt them to become Christians and others retained their belief in the spirit world. For instance my maternal grandfather stayed pagan while my father was a very staunch Protestant who, when he returned home at the end of World War II, became a founder member of St Bartholomew, the village church of Amaohuru (my natural mother's village).

So my name was added to the list of confirmation candidates and I started attending classes which went on for 2 or 3 months. Towards the end of this period I did something to infuriate Jemima. I was a member of the youth club in my village and, since I was very outgoing and persuasive, I had agreed to go round with the secretary on a recruiting drive for new members. The secretary had a bicycle and I was going to sit on the back pannier on the trip round the village and surroundings. He had arrived to pick me up just at the moment Jemima had told me to go and collect firewood for the evening's cooking. I was annoyed as there was already enough wood and I felt she was doing this intentionally to spite me. I snapped and walked out, jumping on the bicycle and we rode away.

Jemima was obviously furious, thinking, as she usually did, that I was defying her in order to go off enjoying myself with a boy. By way of revenge she decided that she would destroy my chances of being confirmed and reported me to the Catechist, telling him that she did not think I was ready to be a candidate. This was her chance to teach me a lesson once and for all.

We were always at each other's throats. During our fights she would often say, "You are a bad child, you killed your mother and your father."

She knew this was not true but I would cry non-stop for days, just praying for death to take me away. But I did give back as much as I could.

On one occasion I said to her, "As I killed both my parents, and you know I am a bad child, you are going to die like them, since I will not leave my father's compound because I want to see your dead body taken back to your father's compound just like my mother's was. Then I will get married and there will be nobody to give me any more pain."

This actually silenced her for a while and I think she became worried that I would never leave and probably carry out my threat. The other villagers noticed this and suggested that she should present me with a white goat as a sign of peace.

Anyway, the first I heard of my confirmation rejection was the next Sunday in church when the Catechist stood up to announce that everybody would be disappointed to hear that our daughter, Irene Chioma Oparaji, would not be a candidate at the forthcoming Confirmation ceremony. I was stunned and, after it had sunk in, stood up, and in front of the congregation tore off my chorister's cap and gown, threw them down on the floor of the church and stormed out crying bitterly. I had 2 pennies for the collection and told myself that God was not going to get them for allowing the world to conspire against me.

As I stumbled from the church I promised to myself that if no one called me back to apologise I would spend the 2d on a box of matches. While buying the matches at a stall in the market square, tears streaming down my face, I became convinced that no one cared. Nobody spoke to me or bothered to ask why I was so unhappy so I took this as the indication that God would approve of anything I did. I made my mind up that, if that was the case, then I would make sure that the other confirmation candidates would know what it was like to be an orphan, having to beg for food, shelter, clothes and, most importantly, love.

I ran out of the village to my parent's grave which I had never visited before having been too scared to do this. My mother and father were

buried together in the same plot and, as I stood before it, I told them
that I had not asked to be born and threw myself on the grave, weeping
bitterly. I said out loud that everyone was using me as a football, passing
me to one another for their own convenience. The worst thing was not
being able to confide in anyone. I was the only orphan in the village of
Ezuhu Nguru and I had never encountered any other parentless child
while living at home. As far as I knew I was the only orphan in my age
group and this affected my mental processes badly. This led me to believe
that I was different from others and destined to be a permanent outcast.

Still no one approached me to help or enquire about my state. I told
God that if he was worthy of my worship then he should give me a sign
which I could interpret as meaning the action of removing me from
communion by the Catechist was correct and, although seemingly unfair,
I should accept it. This would have prevented the action that I was about
to embark upon.

God did not speak or act so I continued, in my blind rage, out of the
cemetery and on to the Catechist's house. I arrived, and after making sure
no one was around, struck a match and started to set alight the thatched
eaves of the building. I struck more matches and lit more points around
the whole building. Rapidly the blaze erupted and flames and smoke leapt
into the sky so I ran to hide in the nearby bush to watch it burn. The house
didn't last long and within 10 minutes it started to collapse amid sounds
of cracking and popping. I experienced a feeling of satisfaction at what I
had done—I was convinced I was doing the right thing since I wanted the
Catechist's children to experience homelessness and disruption to their
lives, the same conditions I was living with.

I now turned my attention to the church where the service was
continuing. I had to hurry as the church was 15 minutes from the Catechist's
house and I wanted to hide nearby to make sure the congregation had all
left before I did the same thing to the symbol of God.

As the service finished and the people filed out I waited and watched
until they had all gone. I checked that there was no one left inside. I
couldn't reach the eaves of the church as they were higher than the
Catechist's house so I dragged some bricks which were stacked nearby to
build a platform from which I could start the fire. I had to work quickly
to move my temporary platform around the church so as to start the blaze
evenly.

Immediately after I had got this going I walked away into the bush and circled around, before approaching the church from a different direction, joining people who had come to see the source of the smoke. The crowd grew and after a while others arrived who had been watching the first fire and word spread that something terrible was happening to Protestant property. I stood among them listening to their excitable chatter and eventually made the decision to leave as some of the onlookers were from the congregation. It would not be long before they connected the incidents with me.

I went home and, in my troubled mental state, the only person I could think of turning to was my maternal grandfather, who was about 100 and lived in my mother's village of Amaohuru Nguru. I had occasionally confided in him since the death of my other grandfather and, despite his great age and frailty, he was the only other surviving relative left of any importance to me. He was too old to really help or protect me from the harsh treatment I received from the other adults and, anyway, lived too far away, but talking to him always calmed me. He knew that I was not loved, or even liked, by the others in my compound and that I never played with the other children. He had given me a carved wooden doll which had become my only friend. It went everywhere with me and I clutched it to myself as a source of comfort. I still have this doll which has stayed with me as a constant reminder of my turbulent childhood.

My wooden doll given to me by my grandfather.
This has been with me always and has protected and
comforted me through all my trials and tribulations.

The actions of setting buildings alight was a step further and may seem extreme, but in my childish frustration I was now capable of anything. In fact the 'little devil' that I had become was born out of a combination of fearlessness, shamelessness and bloody mindedness which had been provoked by the way I had been treated by those who only cared for what they could get out of me. In their minds I shouldn't be alive as I should not have survived the death of my mother.

So I went and told my grandfather what I had done.

I said, "I have burned the Catechist's house and his church and they (the people) can go and ask God why this has happened."

He looked perplexed and asked me why I had I done this

"I don't need to tell you," I replied, "you should know why, so they can come to you and ask that question."

"I don't understand why people go to church and lie to themselves and others," I added.

My grandfather, being a pagan, didn't know what to say and called for one of his sons, by the name of De-Nnaji, to get to the bottom of the story. At this moment word about the fires arrived at the compound. This had already been exaggerated into the fact that the whole village was on fire, causing even more consternation.

Jemima, in the meantime, had returned from church not knowing anything about the fires. She had cooked lunch but excluded me due to my behaviour in church during the service. Then she had had her afternoon siesta, woke, and set off to the church for the evening service with my stepbrothers. To make my life more difficult she had locked the house door, even though she still did not know what had happened. They returned soon after and, of course, by now knew everything, having found the church in ruins.

She found that I had broken the lock on the door, had opened the chop box (a large container for storing food) and had eaten as much as I could, destroying the rest by pouring sand over it. She was now feeling scared as she could see how demonic I had become. I must have been a frightening sight to behold due to my state of mind and any slight aggravation could push me over the edge.

However, Jemima, with her usual insensitivity, couldn't resist starting a tirade at me about the destruction. That was the catalyst. I physically attacked her with fists, feet, pieces of firewood, anything I could put my hands on. She tried to fight back but I had the strength of my convictions and the fight only lasted a few minutes before Jemima broke down. I still felt completely justified in my actions and was convinced that God would understand. I reasoned that He had given me the power to do what I thought was correct and, from this moment, I became much stronger and more fearless. In fact this incident helped to further my resolve in order to cope with the many difficulties and obstacles which still lay ahead.

Of course, everyone came to know that I had committed the crimes, and in any case I had told my grandfather. He was very protective of me and kept the villagers away for as long as he could. Many, though, came to see me saying such things as, "Hey, bad baby, why did you burn the church down," calling me witch, evil child and many other names. I responded by saying, "You write a letter to God and get a reply, then you'll find out why I did it." I didn't care what I said as I knew I had nothing to lose any more. Nobody in the village wanted to know me. No official action was taken against me since the only punishment for a child of my age was a beating, and I was quite used to that anyway. So I was left alone.

The sequel to these events is that, many years later, in 1979, I returned to rebuild St Bartholomew's and was married there to my lovely white English 59 year old husband, Lister, a professor I subsequently met. By then I was, in the jargon of the West, a celebrity in my home district and could, with satisfaction, say that God had finally proved Himself to me. But that is another story and another time. What I wasn't to know, then, was that He hadn't quite finished with me yet.

Shortly after my fire raising activities I left the compound to go and stay with my friend, Virginia, who lived in the next village. I worked for my keep by helping Virginia's mum. She had several small farms and a buka (a cafe in a small hut) two miles away in the town of Aboh. I split my time between the buka and the farms but I was uneasy as I was too close to my village Ezuhu Nguru The villagers were convinced that I was possessed by spirits and were hostile towards me. I despised them as they lied about me, exaggerating and inventing stories in order to magnify my evil image. The most hurtful lie, the one that haunted me wherever my background was known, was that I had killed my mother. I was never allowed to forget that. I was not allowed to associate with girls of my own age, although there were a few kind women who did help me, out of pity. Even today there are children in Nigeria who, because of rumours, become excluded from society and live in daily fear. I was lucky in that I was never threatened with death because of my 'sins'. Most children who suffer in this way do not have parents to give meaning to their existence, and only the strong survive.

Aged 13, back row left, with 3 aunties and my cousin
Everest. Just before I joined the Biafran Army in 1967.

I soon left Ezuhu Nguru to go and live with another friend, Maria, in a village 9 miles away. This, at least, put more distance between me and my persecutors. Maria lived with her mother, who was a sister of one of my uncle's wives, in a tiny one roomed shack. Unusually, Maria's mother loved me very much and had told me that my father had been very kind and generous to her and others. She was very poor, with no income, and often there was nothing to eat. Sometimes we were lucky when chickens escaped from adjacent houses and we caught and killed them, making sure that all the residual evidence was cleaned up and buried. It was a very hand to mouth existence.

Because of the tensions caused by this poverty I eventually fell out with Maria. She and I used to pick dried palm kernel growing wild, bring them home to crack and fry, and make black oil for medicinal purposes.

The oil extracted by this process is very rich and is a good medicine for coughs, convulsions, colds and skin treatment. Both Maria's and my daily harvests were combined for Maria to process at the end of the day. On one occasion I took some of the processed cream that Maria had hidden for herself to rub into my skin. Maria saw this and became very angry, shouting that I should use my own kernels for myself. In fact all the kernels had been jointly picked by both of us so they should have been equally ours. She cursed me loudly and, as I was living in her house, could do nothing about it, except move on.

I began to realise that one answer to my problems would be to find someone in a similar situation to mine. At least we could share the stigma and rejection together. I had a friend called Florence who lived with a stepmother who had recently married her father following the death of his wife. I went to see her at her house in the village of Obetiti and she was overjoyed to see me. We spent all night sitting on her bed, talking. I recounted to her all that had happened to me since we last had met and I found that we had much in common. We were both free-spirited and generally unloved. Florence was extremely unhappy with the atmosphere in the house since her father had little time for her now that he had a new wife. The stepmother was very unpleasant towards her and her father was not good at diplomacy.

I knew this scenario very well.

We talked about running away to join the Biafran army. The war with the government forces from the north was escalating and most of the young men had disappeared—taken on as conscripts. Only rich families could bribe their sons out of call-up. Evidence of the war in Obetiti took the form of air raid sirens and constant aircraft flying over the area. At this time the front line was about 30 miles away.

Florence had some reservations about leaving home this way, since, unlike my situation, she still had a natural father and, if our plans failed, she might have to return, with embarrassing consequences. Nevertheless we took steps to prepare ourselves should we decide to go. As we were both 13 we knew we were too young to join as buffs (the name given to potential spies or scouts, a job that was normally carried out by 18 year-olds), so we started working out how we could make ourselves look older. This took a bit of time and initiative. We had no money so we went to the market to try and steal some items that were required for this purpose. What we needed were brassieres, cotton wool, panties, powder, eye pencil, lipstick, etc. While one of us distracted the trader the other was picking what she could.

When we got home we tried making up to look like ladies. We enlarged our pre-pubescent breasts with limes wrapped in cotton wool and, after much practice, we eventually felt comfortable enough. We made up our faces and the results of our efforts made us look at least 4 or 5 years older. We were ready to go and Florence decided that anything was better than staying at home.

One evening, before Florence's stepmother had returned from the market where she worked, we left carrying our disguises and hitch-hiked in the direction of Umuahia where we had been told the forces selection point was located. The distance was only about 25 miles but it took us 3 days to get there, We begged for food on the way but this was often unsuccessful, so stealing became the main source of sustenance.

CHAPTER 6

Military Training

When we got close to the selection centre we went off the road into the bush to change into our new characters before joining the queue of applicants. There were many girls as most of the boys had already been conscripted and sent for rapid training and deployment to the front line. Florence and I split up and queued in different lines so as not to be identified together. After about 45 minutes I reached the head of my line where there were a group of uniformed officers. Some were sitting at desks and some standing.

"Why are you here?" said one of the standing officers.

"I would like to be out there helping my brothers, even if it is only cooking food and washing pots for them," I replied, trying to sound confident.

He waved me through and I had to restrain myself from jumping in excitement. It was like passing an exam. However, I was concerned for Florence as she had not yet reached the officers at the head of her line. I was worried that if she was turned back she would have to return home alone and it would have all been my fault. I was more worried for her than myself since I would have been no worse off had I failed. As I was moved forward to the next stage I came to a group of recruits sitting on the ground waiting for instructions. I looked back to try and see how Florence was getting on. Then I saw her being motioned through by an officer with a swagger stick. She came over and sat next to me. We were overjoyed and excited that we were about to find a reason for our existence. I can still remember the feeling of euphoria at the prospect of suddenly having a meaningful life ahead of me. Florence and I had often discussed getting to this stage where our elders wouldn't matter anymore. We had both agreed that a bullet was much more preferable than the constant pain our lives had been up to this point.

What I couldn't know then was that Florence would not survive the war. But at that time neither of us cared about survival.

After the initial selection process had been completed we were asked for our details. Neither of us had any identification, but it didn't matter as no papers or documents were required. We gave our names and our ages as 18 which was the minimum requirement, we didn't dare try to make it any older. An officer ordered us to stand and get into line. Names were called and we had to shout "Here, sir" and raise our hands when we heard it. Then an officer explained why we were there, and what would happen next.

Then we were taken to the mess hall which was full of tables and chairs and we queued up to collect our first meal. A vivid memory I have of this meal was my surprise at tasting salt again. For at least a year I had gone without it because of its scarcity and exorbitant price. When the meal was over we went to the accommodation blocks. The beds were 3 tier bunks in a hall housing about 100 of us. I was intoxicated by a mixture of excitement and wonder—this was a whole new world for me and, so far, it had been surprisingly easy to get into.

Florence and I were together throughout the induction process and our beds were not very far apart in the barrack block, so we were able to talk and compare our feelings at each stage of this new experience. Under each 3 bunk column was a 3 section wooden container for our belongings and equipment, one for each bunk. I packed my few belongings in my box—these included the wooden doll given to me by my maternal grandfather, a hymn book given to me by my brother, Emmanuel, and a beaded rope which I had always worn round my waist, and still do. I had worn this bead rope from a very young age as a substitute for clothing in the compound, running around naked as the other children did. These three items were never far from my side and, I believe, have always kept me safe. The doll represented the pagan beliefs of my mother's family and the hymnal stood for my father's Protestant faith. So I was well covered for any eventuality.

Our biggest problems were being in constant contact with so many people and having to conceal the fact that we were so young, We kept our breast enlargements in place for the whole 3 week training period and I had a scare when I fell into a river during one exercise. I had to be pulled out and was lucky not to have my false arrangement discovered.

Each day started with a loud whistle at 4 am. There was no washing in the morning as training started immediately. This consisted of running, jumping between, over, and around obstacles. Then we had breakfast before more training, which lasted all day. We had been issued with uniforms—green camouflaged jacket and trousers, jungle boots and camouflaged bush hat, and a steel helmet. We had two of most items and I began to feel very important. Everything had to be signed for.

The first part of our 3 week training was taken up by physical exercises, followed by instruction on moving around in enemy territory, e.g. crawling and keeping as low a profile as possible. We progressed quickly to the live weapons section and were shown all types including Mk4 rifle, machine gun, mortars, grenades, etc. My personal weapon was to be the Mills hand grenade. We had live firing on the range—"Don't fire aimlessly". Everything was carried out at high speed. It was obvious they were desperate to get us trained and into real live action as the Biafran armed services were tiny compared to the Nigerian forces.

I learned later that the organisation of the Biafran army was far superior to that of the Nigerian government forces and some experts are of the opinion that the war would have lasted much longer if Biafra had had better supply routes.

There were no exams but we were given practice in combat situations to prepare us for hand to hand fighting and methods of killing. My speciality was to be spying and intelligence gathering so I was given instructions on how to move around enemy territory using maps and compass and identifying the locations and size of enemy formations. This was when I came to realise that my role in this war was basically as a civilian with military specialisation. My job, and others like me, was to infiltrate enemy lines posing as civilians in order to gain information on positions and strengths. We operated singly but many of us would cover one particular area leaving bush craft signals to indicate to others where we had been. We were armed only with hand grenades, signed for and buried when we were in the combat zone. These hiding spots had to be strictly referenced and were only known to the individual. If the grenades were not used we recovered and brought them back to be signed back into the armoury.

If the chance arose we were to poison water supplies used by the enemy. The poison was carried under the fingernails of the left hand and was transferred by dipping the hand into the water. Once we had mastered the military techniques we reverted back to being civilians. We were told that we would enter no man's land and occupied territory openly and act as locals, even talking to enemy soldiers to gain their confidence. My skill at languages was particularly important to the army, especially the language of the enemy (Hausa).

Florence and I had never enjoyed ourselves so much—without this war we would have continued with our sad and unhappy existences. Initially we hoped it would last forever. What more could we have asked for; we had food in abundance, companionship, excitement, and a feeling of purpose.

As the end of training approached I began to feel tremendous loyalty to the Biafran cause and looked forward to going on my first operation. We were given lectures on the reasons for the war and it was explained to us that it was mainly over oil. Biafra in the East had the oil whereas in the North and West there was no oil. Biafran leaders resented the taking of our natural wealth without much in return and this eventually boiled over into open hostility. However, there was more to it than that. Our leader Major General. Dim Ojukwu was adored after the summit of African leaders held at Oburi, Ghana in January 1967. The slogan at this summit was "On Oburi (we stand)", but he opposed the concept of a Biafra within Nigeria and, when he returned, the phrase, "On Biafra we stand", was born. Our favourite wartime song went like this:

"Iwe neweme Iwe Iwe neweme iwe (x2)
Ojukwu yem Egbe Kam ga gide Gowon Naka
Ojukwu yem Egbe Kam ga gide Hassan Naka"

Which translates as:

"I am angry, I am angry, Ojukwu should give me the gun and, with my hands I will capture Gowon alive; I will capture Hassan alive."

There was a big passing out parade at the end of training with a band and we marched past the reviewing officer giving him an 'eyes right'. Florence and I had trained together and we had also learned army parade drill as well as combat techniques. I can still execute all my drill movements. It's like riding a bicycle, you never forget it. Unfortunately we were posted to different camps and I never saw her again. I have often thought of her over the years but never found out what happened to her. She may even be still alive, but in the turmoil of the conflict and Biafran defeat, with many hundreds of thousands dying and displaced, I may never find out.

CHAPTER 7

Active Service

I was posted with two other girls to 133 Battalion, a forward camp at Imerienwe about 40 miles from the training camp. My arrival was greatly appreciated because I could speak Hausa (the Northern language) fluently as well my own Igbo tongue. This made me useful when talking to, or interrogating, the enemy. On arrival we were welcomed by a female corporal (the buffs did not normally display their ranks) and we were shown round the camp, which was a converted boarding school called Nnanna-Ukaegbu's College.

Without delay we were taken into the common room and given a lecture on the current situation and the position of the enemy. We were told to be on immediate standby for any eventuality and it was confirmed that our role would be reconnaissance and intelligence gathering. We were also warned that we would be on our own during missions into no-man's land or enemy territory and, if we were caught or wounded, it would be up to us to get ourselves out of any situation. We were never to admit any connection with Biafra. Deny everything!

One important rule was to do with timing. On each operation we would be given a limit on how long we should be away. This varied according to the distance of the location from the camp and the nature of the work. If we were very late back or did not come back at all then it would be assumed that we had been captured or killed. If we were captured, and then escaped, we would be written off and not employable by the Biafran forces in the future. This was because many people changed sides, sometimes more than once, and these were known as saboteurs. It was a problem for the commanders and they took no chances.

Special equipment for the girls included panties with an inner side pocket containing gauze, cotton wool, and surgical blades. This was to be used for protection against sexual demands. Hausa belief is that a woman in her period is dirty and untouchable. The equipment issued was used to simulate this condition by making a cut, say a finger, dabbing the cotton wool in the blood and placing this in the pants. We were told that this would be enough to deter any would be assailant, or admirer. Some could be persistent but the sight of blood in the right place normally dampened their enthusiasm. We dressed in old worn clothing and carried one hand grenade in a bag, and a compass. The grenade was to be used only as a last resort and was buried soon after we entered no-man's land. We could then return to unearth it if we thought we might need it, and we always brought it back if it was unused.

All our operations were carried out on foot. On leaving the secure area we were issued with a code to pass through the sentry post. On our return the sentry would call out, "Halt, who is there?" and we would reply, "Friend", putting our hands up. If he recognised us we would then shout the code back to him and, if satisfied, he would give the order for us to advance.

At last the day of my first active operation came. We were under constant air attack from the Nigerians. The camp was camouflaged as much as possible and we escaped much of the bombing, but the civilian population suffered badly. Most attacks were on market places and houses which were easily seen from the air. This was my first experience of the carnage of war and unburied bodies littered the countryside. If there was time corpses were buried in large pits but these were shallow and marked by bloated hands and feet poking out where animals had been active. I soon became unconcerned by the sights of war.

On return from a reconnaissance operation we would be taken into the de-briefing room for about 2 hours to give details of enemy positions which were plotted on maps for use in planning attacks. Also notes were made of the people we had met during the mission. I was always very accurate with my reports and most attacks based on my information were highly successful. I came to be known as 'Last Card'. If an area was considered particularly difficult or dangerous the officers would call for Last Card to be sent in. In contrast some spies were not very effective and often just made up stories when they found some areas too difficult, or they became frightened and wanted to get back to the camp.

I can honestly say that I was never frightened by anything I encountered during this period of my life and wondered why I felt this way. I think it may have been because I had been brought up to believe in my reputation as an 'evil' child. It certainly helped to be this way in these circumstances and I had a very tough reputation. After all I was still hoping that I would die—smoking was not working so maybe this occupation would do the job for me. As I became more experienced I was given heavier workloads and employed on more dangerous assignments.

I worked in many areas during the latter half of 1967 and 1968 but on one occasion in early 1969 I was sent to Owerri area, which I obviously knew very well, to carry out an investigation into enemy strengths. While I was burying my equipment (hand grenade, compass, etc.) in no-man's land I noticed smoke up ahead indicating that people were close. I moved towards the smoke and eventually came upon a house with two girls standing outside. They were very surprised to see me as they said that all the local people had run away. The girls looked healthy and well dressed and told me they had stayed to look after their grandparents who hadn't wanted to move. I told them I was wandering alone in the bush trying to get away from my family with whom I had fallen out. To gain their sympathy I said that I was fed up with hiding in the bush, occasionally coming out to get food, and was trying to get captured or killed.

One of the girls said, "Don't worry they won't do anything to you. Stay with us and we'll look after you."

They told me that Nigerian officers, who had become their boyfriends, would be coming soon from Aba to pick them up after their work was finished, and would take them to their camp. The girls said there was no problem with this and the Nigerians were good and decent towards them. They were given anything they asked for and said the officers were very critical of Ojukwu whom they blamed for this stupid war. I pretended to look interested to keep them happy and waited with them for the soldiers to arrive. Luckily, I had been given 24 hours for this assignment but I didn't want to overshoot this. I was always very conscious of my timing as I didn't want to be branded a saboteur and lose my job. I was totally loyal to my country and its cause and would never have changed sides but my commanders would not know that.

The girls gave me a decent dress and made me look nice for the Nigerian officers. They arrived at the exact time the girls predicted and were surprised to see me, excited at a new girl, and said that I would be good for one of their friends. The girls told them that I was one of their sisters and they accepted me without question. We were driven off quickly as the soldiers were breaking rules by being in no-man's land. We arrived at their camp and I was introduced to the friend who was called Muasa. He was very likeable and took to me immediately. We stayed the night and I used my period kit to avoid having to have sex with him. He was good about this and didn't touch me.

We were told that we would have to be dropped off in no-man's land very early next morning, which suited me as I calculated that I had about 4 hours to get back to my camp in order to be within the 24 hour limit.

When we arrived back at their house the girls said that I could see there was no danger. The Nigerians were only after Biafran armed forces, and civilians were safe. They suggested that I should go and get my friends, which I had told them I had, as the Nigerians wanted more girls. I pretended to agree and set off telling them that I would be back. On the way I collected my buried equipment and managed to get back to my camp with 1½ hours to spare.

At the de-brief where many clerks took notes, and maps were scrutinised, I told the commanders my story and they were impressed. I had got a lot of information from Muasa and others about Nigerian strengths of personnel and equipment in this area. They had boasted that they had enough firepower and men to wipe out the Biafran forces facing them. In fact they said that there was to be a heavy attack in 2 days on the area in which my camp was situated and had even named Nnanna Ukaegbu College, our battalion HQ. Obviously Biafran deserters (saboteurs) had given them this information. This presented the commanders with a dilemma and they had to act fast. I said that I would like to capture the Nigerian officers so we could extract more information from them. I was asked how I intended to do this and told them that I could set up an ambush with 12 men as there were plenty of bushes around the girl's compound. The commander said 12 were too many and he would assign me only 7, warning me that if I lost any I needn't come back.

The senior officer then said to the others, "You all know what Last Card can do. Get the men organised and get started immediately."

So the operation was set up for that evening, to tie in with my arrangement to meet the girls I had befriended. I had only just arrived back from no-man's land, been de-briefed, and had not eaten. Yet now I was to return with a seven man team for a high precision strike on the enemy. I was so excited that I didn't feel like eating and could only concentrate on the preparations for the operation. A sergeant brought the armed Biafran soldiers to me in the compound, where they had 15 minutes practice and instruction in moving through the bush in single file, 5 yards apart and keeping cover from the enemy. I was to walk towards the compound along the track fully visible but occasionally moving into the bush to confuse any enemy sentries.

I signed for 7 men, weapons and ammunition and we were ready to go. We had to be at the girls' house at 6pm and it was nearly 3pm already. As it was 8 miles to the house we had to leave immediately.

We got near to the compound at about 5-30pm and my soldiers took up ambush positions. I walked up to the house and the sisters greeted me.

"Where are your friends?" they asked in unison.

"The stupid girls didn't believe me when I told them that they would like the Nigerians, "I replied, "so I had to come on my own."

They looked disappointed and said that my friends would be the losers.

We waited for the arrival of the Nigerian officers and when they came they got out of their Landrover and went to say hello to the girls' grandparents. Then they went straight to the girls' room where we drank palm wine which the grandfather had produced. My friend Muasa was there and he was very pleased to see me. There were 3 Nigerian soldier escorts and they had got out of the vehicle to accompany the officers to the compound. Then they went into the public room to chat to the grandparents.

The officers were disappointed that I had not brought my friends but I told them I would try and persuade them to come next time. At this point I made some excuse and left the girls' room to see where the Nigerian escorts were. They were completely off guard and had left their rifles against the wall so as not to frighten the grandparents. That was my moment—I knew this was the time to act. My soldiers had crept closer to the compound and I gave them the signal to attack.

Immediately, my seven Biafran comrades rushed into the compound, seized the 3 rifles and ordered the escorts to raise their hands and move out of the public room. Then the Nigerian officers were dealt with in a similar fashion and all seven were quickly lined up ready for return to our camp. The grandparents were put in the Landrover with the captured weapons and driven to the camp. The rest (7 Nigerians and 3 girls, myself included in order to keep up the illusion that I was on their side) were marched away, prodded along by the Biafran soldiers.

We reached our camp quickly and, as the Landrover had already arrived, report of our success had already spread. To the astonishment of the captives I was lifted on to the shoulders of my colleagues and paraded around to the joyful singing of our war song:

Iwe neweme O Iwe Iwe neweme O Iwe
Ojukwu yem Egbe Kam ga gide Gowon Naka
Ojukwu yem Egbe Kam ga gide Hassan Naka

It was the proudest moment of my life to that point. For once I was the heroine, not the downtrodden, abused, depressed child which I was accustomed to being. At last I had time to relax—all the officers kept on congratulating me and the story of the operation was told and re-told. Then a senior officer came up to me, made a speech and announced that I was promoted to the field rank of Sergeant. Of course I couldn't wear the stripes as we were special forces, but I was a Sergeant nevertheless.

The captured Nigerians were locked up that evening, prior to interrogation, and I didn't see them again that day. I went to bed and slept soundly, bathed in the warm feeling that comes with success and the admiration of others. However, next morning I was interested in seeing the prisoners and to find out how they were adjusting to their new surroundings.

I was taken to the cell block by the duty officer and warned that I shouldn't stand too close to the bars. They were all in one cell, lying or sitting, and looking very dejected. When they became aware of my presence they got up and came to the door.

Muasa, who had been very keen on me, said in the Northern language, "Hey, pretty girl, why did you do this to me? You must be really heartless.

I thought I was friends with a human being, not knowing that you were my enemy—that is shocking."

I replied with feeling, "Why did you come here to kill my brothers? What did you expect?"

He answered, "If I am conscripted to join an army, trained, given a gun and sent to fight I have to obey."

I told him that I didn't care for life anymore as all my brothers had been killed by Nigerians and that I am doing what is right for Biafra. We had a long conversation and then I left feeling confident that I had done my duty. I now wanted to see the girls whom I had used in the operation. They were being kept in a room, not in prison, as it had been accepted that they were not actively involved in helping the enemy.

They were surprised to see me and cried out, "Hey, Chioma, we wish we were like you. We couldn't believe that you were doing this work. You must be a very strong girl."

I couldn't tell whether they were indicating that they would like to join us or whether they were just trying to make things easy for themselves.

So I replied, "It is lucky you were nice to me, otherwise you would now be in the same cell as your boyfriends."

I told them that I had just seen them and, although the girls asked how they were, they made sure that I was not given the impression that they cared for their welfare. I said the officers were being questioned and I didn't know what would happen to them, which was true. I also said that if the girls behaved themselves they might be trained to do similar work. I actually felt quite sorry for them as they were in this situation because they had stayed to look after their grandparents.

Two days later, following their interrogation, I went back to see the captured Nigerians. The major attack which they had boasted about had taken place but it was unsuccessful and we had pushed them back from their positions by a couple of miles. The information I had been instrumental in obtaining was beneficial in preventing our defeat. (This was typical of many similar situations involving intelligence gathering. The war, which lasted about 3 years, would have been much shorter but for the activities of spies and counter spies. It was a very dirty conflict and no one really knew who their true friends were. Many people changed sides more than once to suit their situation at the time).

I was now in for a shock. The prisoners had been interrogated and it had been decided that as much information as possible had been obtained. I didn't know if torture had been applied as no one had spoken to me about the details of their questioning. As I approached their cell where I expected to see them, I felt a bit apprehensive but I wasn't ready for the sight that greeted me. On the ground outside the cell door was a wooden plank, on which was placed a row of heads, neatly spaced and all pointing in the same direction. I was overcome by this moment. I had known these people and, even if they were the enemy, I had been the main factor in their capture. I still have nightmares of this and other gruesome events that I experienced during this war.

The reason the heads were kept was to provide proof of their capture to HQ. A further disturbing by-product of the war was, that due to near starvation of the civilians in the areas of conflict, cannibalism was sometimes practiced. So that when it became known that captured enemy were being held, villagers started hanging around the camp gates for when the bodies of the executed were dumped.

A few weeks after my military success, I was transferred permanently to Owerri which was under attack after the fall of Aba. The Nigerians were advancing rapidly from village to village, but Owerri was strongly defended since it was a focal town for both sides and had become a major factor in the struggle. Owerri had been attacked twice before and had only been saved by a combination of savage hand to hand fighting and the poisoning of the enemy's drinking water by recce girls like me.

During the second offensive I was captured while on a mission. Two soldiers became suspicious of me and started asking questions. They suspected that I was up to no good and took me to their camp in Nekede which had been my destination. I was put into a bunker which held four buff girls who had already been interrogated for several days. Each day we were taken out and tortured in order to extract information about our activities. This went on for about 4 days which exceeded my operational limit of 24 hours. This meant that I was written off by my company as missing, presumed dead or absconded and, subsequently would be considered a traitor (or saboteur) if I returned. I had no intention of changing sides as my loyalty to the cause was unshakeable, but they were not to know that and there had been painful instances where trust had backfired, so there were no exceptions.

The torture was employed if it was assumed that information was being withheld. After minor infliction of pain it was increased to the extent of making prisoners eat parts of their bodies (fingers, ears, breasts) before throwing them back into the bunker to think about it. Before interrogation started the Nigerian guards took pleasure in warning us what the day's particular activity would be. This alone was often enough to extract what they wanted.

When I arrived the other girls had been in captivity for a week and were ready for the advanced treatment. They had been through the beatings stage but, although I had been there for a shorter period, I suspected that I would soon be given the advanced treatment. When the captain came in one morning to give the order for the day's torture programme, I was convinced I was about to start the slow death process. I pretended to panic and started babbling in Hausa (the Northern language) that I lived with my brother who was in the Nigerian army in barracks in Zaria (North Nigeria), and begged to be sent back there to be with him. I gave the captain details of my brother's address. This seemed to work as he appeared sympathetic and recognized the address I gave him. He gave an order to the guards to move me from the bunker to his office.

Later he came into his office and made me repeat everything I had said in the cell. We were conversing in Hausa which appeared to impress him, as very few people in Eastern Nigeria speak this language as fluently as I do. This may have made him think I was a Northern Nigerian. After he had noted down everything I had told him he said that he would hold me for 4 days in Nekede and then would send me to Port Harcourt, and from there to my brother in Zaria. What he didn't know was that my brother, Ambrose, had already left Zaria and had joined the Biafran army.

The captain gave an order to the guards to move me from the bunker to his quarters and I began to feel confident about surviving my capture. During the following days I worked out a plan which involved escaping from the Nigerians and returning to my comrades in the Biafran camp at Imerienwe. I would take my chances with them despite the ruling governing the overrunning of the time limit on operations. In any case I couldn't go back to Zaria as they would discover that my brother had deserted the Nigerian army, and then I would be in big trouble.

I reckoned it would easy to escape from the Nigerian camp as I was not guarded and I was a familiar figure by now. I picked my moment when the camp was emptier than usual due to the beginning of a big offensive on Owerri. Only the guards were left so I walked to the gate quite openly where the sentry stopped me. I told him I was going for a walk and he waved me through. I walked casually until I thought I was out of the guard's sight then I went into the bush and proceeded in the direction of Imeriewue.

After a while I reached a point where I had to cross the main Aba—Owerri road. The problem was crossing without being noticed by the Nigerian Observation Posts. There had been intensive fighting in this area and there were bodies and limbs in various stages of decay lying all over the place, on the road and in the bush. I tried to make myself look like an animal and hopped across the road. I don't know what animal I was supposed to be, but it seemed to work as no one shouted at me. On the other side of the road I walked for a bit, and then sat down to gather my thoughts together. I was hungry so I sang a song to myself:

> "Anam gla ni iwe, Anam ala niwe onye a gbajikwelem ukwu dead body ewe ukwu ewaka naka aga nime ohia je biri, ammem amutalom pomu soldier bi ni me ohia agurd agugbole nu wa mama ewe ewe

Which translates as:

> The dead body has got no strength in its feet or hands and my mum had me and called me an animal soldier in the bush, the hunger is torturing the mother's child so I'm angry and angry.

As it was late I made a bed of leaves under a tree and slept. Next morning at sunrise I got up and continued on my way. I reached a dead river of stagnant water covered in leaves so I slid down the bank until I reached a tree hanging from the opposite bank. I climbed up the branches and crossed on the trunk and jumped down on to the other bank. At that moment I detected a pungent smell. There was a track, not human, which I traced to the river I had just crossed, then I noticed a stick with a bowl shaped leaf attached, which made me think that a human was in the area.

I walked back, re-tracing my steps along the track, when suddenly I noticed a man who looked like a chimpanzee sitting on a mattress of leaves. He was naked and both his legs were missing from above the knees—the stumps were white with pus, but apart from his appearance he acted quite normally.

He greeted me with, "Hello little girl, where are you coming from?"

"What are you doing here?" I replied, uneasily.

He told me that he was Nigerian and he had been involved in a battle with the Biafrans. They had left him as they thought he was dead, but he had survived for, "I don't know how long." He couldn't tell me anymore except to ask me to tell someone he was there. I didn't go close to him as he might have grabbed me, so I left him and continued on my way.

It took me a day to get to my camp at Imerienwe and when I arrived I was immediately arrested as a suspected saboteur, having been away for 12 days on a 24 hour mission. I was questioned and due to my previous record was given the benefit of the doubt. However, they said I could not continue in my role as a spy and gave me leave; in other words they weren't interested in me anymore. I felt very bitter at this and decided that I was finished with the army since I felt betrayed by the people and organisation to which I had given so much loyalty. They drove me 10 miles from the camp and dropped me off at the side of the road to find my own way home. I sat there weeping for hours. I had never experienced such pain despite my harsh life. This was cruelty of a different kind and I could only seek consolation from my wooden doll.

It was October 1969, I was 15, and my army career was now only a memory. In fact, the way it had happened probably saved my life. For, although the war was nearly over, many more were still to die in bitter fighting before the end.

CHAPTER 8

A Soul Saved

So I started walking and after a couple of hours a Landrover passed me and stopped. A Biafran army officer leant out and asked me where I was going and whether I wanted a lift. I accepted and sat in the front with him. He asked me what I was doing on my own in that area, so I told him as much as I dared and said that I had just been discharged from the Biafran army which seemed to interest him very much. He then told me he was on his way to 168 Battalion where many had been killed or wounded. He was going to Uruala where all the casualties had been taken. It happened that one of my brothers, Emmanuel, was serving in 168 Battalion so I asked the officer if I could go with him and he agreed. When we arrived I went to the hospital straight away and while the officer, whose name was Aaron, was looking for casualties from his family I started looking for someone who might have news of Emmanuel.

The situation in the hospital was appalling. The main wards were full and, with many hundreds of wounded men, all the corridors, storerooms, in fact any available space, was being used. The patients were lying on the floors and very little effort was being taken to make them comfortable, let alone treat their wounds.

After walking round the complex several times I noticed that the big toe of one patient was looking very familiar. I called my brother's name and the owner of the toe responded by looking up and giving me a ghostly smile. He had recognised me but was unable to say much as he was badly wounded and covered in sores which were infested with maggots. I stayed by the bench, which was his bed, for a few minutes and cried. Then I went to find Aaron to tell him that I wanted to stay and help since the patients were dying, not only from their injuries but also from hunger and lack of water.

Aaron agreed to this and we went to a nearby village where I rented a room so I could base myself close to the hospital. I then bought some food, cotton wool, disinfectant, powder and a flask and returned quickly to the hospital to start the job of healing my brother. He was so hungry that he almost gulped down the spoon as I fed him. With my limited resources I bathed his wounds and sores and helped with others. Some of the wounded had suffered horrific injuries and wouldn't stand much chance of survival but we had to try and do what we could.

After about 2 weeks Emmanuel began to improve and when we got him to his feet I had to teach him how to walk again. For me it was a miracle that he could walk at all because, when I had first seen him, I never believed he would ever recover but, as God would have it, he recovered very quickly. I stayed in Uruala for a month and by the end of this period he was able to walk unaided. His injuries which had consisted of bullet and shrapnel wounds over much of his body, coupled with shell shock from the resulting trauma, would take much longer to fully heal, if at all. I befriended the few nurses working in this place to try and ensure that he got the best possible attention. Other patients were less fortunate and many died, while I was there, from lack of medicine and care. I didn't see many other visitors which was depressing for them.

When Emmanuel was in a good enough state to leave I decided that the best place for him was back in our village. I was fortunate in this decision since Aaron, who had returned to his battalion, came back to see how I was getting on. I think he was interested in me, but the circumstances for romance were not conducive, and he behaved like a perfect gentleman. He was surprised and impressed at Emmanuel's revival and I told him that I was ready to take him home. Aaron was pleased to be able to help and offered to drive us to Mbaise.

I said goodbye to the nurses, some of whom I had got to know very well, and we climbed into the Land Rover for the journey home. Emmanuel, who had been transformed from a living corpse into a reasonably healthy person was excited at the prospect of going back to his village with the sister he never thought he would see again.

On arrival at the Ezuhu Nguru family compound Aaron dropped us off and, being the decent man he was, gave me some money to tide us over. He said he would come back on Sunday, and left. Most of the people still living in the village were either very old or very young—those not actively involved in the war. They came over to welcome us after Aaron had gone and to hear the story of how I came to be bringing my brother home. Emmanuel was in no condition to say very much so I did most of the talking. Jemima was still there, as ever, she had last seen me when I was a child, but she had lost none of her vindictiveness towards me. After I finished my tale she couldn't resist the old feelings of jealousy and bitterness and said, in a reference to my experiences, "Being Ojukwu's daughter I have no doubt Chioma can do anything." I ignored the sarcasm, realising that nothing had changed, and turned my attention towards the immediate future.

I went to the local market and with the money Aaron had given me, bought enough provisions to ensure that Emmanuel would be comfortable and able to continue his journey towards full health. Aaron came back on Sunday as he had promised and I went with him to his camp. We went to his quarters where I met many of his fellow officers. He introduced me as his wife and I felt very comfortable in his presence. In fact, if he had asked me to marry him I would probably have done so, but the war had dislocated normal life. I was 15 and in Nigeria this was not too young to become a bride. The fact of the matter was that Aaron, being a kind man, was more interested in helping me to get over my problems with Emmanuel and the traumas of my military experiences, than in concentrating on our personal relationship.

After a week he took me back to my village so I could be with my brother. He dropped me at the compound entrance and drove off, after saying that he would come and see me a week later. I walked into the compound and was immediately confronted by Jemima who took great delight in shouting, "Ah, here's Ojukwu's daughter. Does she know that they've just taken her brother away?"

"Who's taken him away?" I said, starting to panic.

"Aren't you Ojukwu's daughter?" she replied "You should know that every young man must be away fighting for our country. Anyway I am not your brother's keeper, you should go and tell Ojukwu's boys to return him."

I deduced from her cryptic comments that Biafran soldiers had taken him away. Then some children told me that they had taken him in the direction of Aboh. They said he was among other suspected runaway soldiers who were being rounded up. The problem was that people visiting the village had seen Emmanuel, a young man of fighting age, living amongst children and the elderly so the word had spread. They did not know, or chose to ignore, that he had just escaped death in the service of his country. He had been reported to the nearest army authorities by a diligent citizen.

I dropped my belongings and ran the 1½ miles to Aboh. When I got there I went to the centre and found a large group of men, guarded by armed soldiers. I noticed Emmanuel among them, recognisable by the bandage round his head. I bought him some bananas, oranges and a bag of peanuts and then spoke to the officer in charge of the guards. I told him I was on leave from my unit and asked if he would release my brother into my care. He replied that he could not do that as others were asking the same thing, and he could not create a precedent without his authority being undermined. However, he gave me the address of the camp to which they were taking the prisoners and suggested that I should go up there and explain why my brother should be released.

When I saw the address I was delighted, as it was 168 Battalion—Aaron's unit. I quickly hired a motorbike and rider for £8 to take me to Aaron's camp, so I could get there before the prisoners. I entered the camp using the pass that Aaron had got for me and frantically started looking for him. Luckily he was in the camp and I found him in his office where I blurted out that Emmanuel had been apprehended as a deserter. Aaron assured me that he would sort it out and wrote a note ordering Emmanuel's release on his arrival at the camp and instructions that he should be brought to his quarters. As he was doing this I heard the strains of men singing:

> "Biafra kunie kai laso Nigeria (agha agha agha) x2 (makagini nihina ha bu ndi namaigh chineke ndi namiaigh chuku onye kere ha) x2"

Which is:

> "Bifrans should stand up wherever they are, let's go and fight the Nigerians because they are heartless and wicked and they do not know the God that created them"

The deserters had been coerced into singing in order to either restore their enthusiasm for the war, or to re-instill discipline.

"That must be them now," I said to Aaron.

"Yes, that's the song they make them sing when they come in," he replied.

I asked Aaron if I could hide in his bedroom explaining that I didn't want Emmanuel to see me in his house. Strangely, I was ashamed that my brother might see me with an officer and that he might not approve of my association with an older man. From the bedroom I heard Emmanuel come in and tell Aaron that he had been grabbed by soldiers. Aaron asked him how he felt and he said he was ok. So he was given a 3 month pass, some food and told that no one would bother him for that time. A driver was then instructed to take him back to his village. The whole episode had taken place without him knowing I had been there and had heard everything.

I spent the night in Aaron's quarters and left in the morning after thanking him for all his help. He really was a very pleasant man and, under different circumstances, our friendship could have developed into something deeper. As it was I had to concentrate on making sure my brother was properly re-habilitated and then to start picking up the pieces of my own life. I suspected that Aaron was planning to ask me to marry him, but I had reverted to my anti-marriage attitude and put out a cold front towards him to dissuade him from this idea. He was very easy to handle being such a gentleman. However I was quite prepared to hang on with him until my brother was secure. Emmanuel was safe as long as Aaron was handling his case, since only Aaron knew how close he had been to death and, therefore, not of any use in further fighting.

On my return to the compound my nemesis returned. Jemima appeared in front of me and, putting her face close to mine, she exclaimed in her infantile way, "I knew you were Ojukwu's daughter, you've brought your brother back!"

I ignored her and went to find my brother. He was in high spirits and couldn't believe how he had once again escaped disaster. I told him that he had been very fortunate and to think no more about it.

Now that my duty to Emmanuel was complete and Aaron had promised him that he would not be sent back to the front, I decided to leave the compound and go and visit my friend Regina in Arondizuogo, a village 40 miles from Mbaise. I bade my brother farewell. He was very tearful and appreciative of what I had done for him and this made me very happy, as I loved the feeling of having helped someone in difficulty. I have always felt this way. On the other hand I was not sorry to be leaving Jemima. I often look back on my association with her. At times she had made my life miserable for long periods, but in a strange way I do not now have any hate in my heart for her. I do think that, at that age, I was quite a difficult person and that without her constant tormenting I might have developed differently, possibly worse.

My only surviving brother, Emmanuel.
Taken many years after his rescue from the war.

Despite continual bad luck in my life I am reasonably satisfied at the way I have turned out. I have often imagined that there can be very few things worse than despising one's self for actions taken in the past. Guilt is a continuous process and deepens with advancing age. I like to think

71

my conscience is as clear as it can be. I did make a deliberate decision at this time not to go back to my family because I knew that no one would want to see me since they all thought I was a bad child when I was younger. In fact I stopped going to church due to the behaviour of so-called Christians. They show themselves off as great believers but the most dedicated Christians in my family were the most cruel. The odd thing is that they all knew what they were doing, and that it was not in accordance with the Lord's teachings. But the worst of the lot was my stepmother. She constantly criticised me in front of others, despite the fact that I was popular with most of the parents of my friends. If I was sent to work with other families I worked harder than anyone and was always being asked back. However without parents of my own I was always an outcast at the end of the day.

I told Aaron that I was going away for two weeks to see my friend and he said that he would miss me and looked forward to my return. But I had no intention of returning. Now that my brother was safe I was ready to move on. I never saw Aaron again, although Emmanuel told me that, years later, he came looking for me but nobody knew where I was and he went away. I also learned that all my siblings, over 22 years of age, except Emmanuel, had disappeared, presumed dead, as a result of the war. I am reminded of this terrible purge of human life whenever I hear the words of the old hymn:

> Time, like an ever-rolling stream,
> Bears all its sons away
> They fly, forgotten as a dream,
> Dies at the opening day.

CHAPTER 9

The Search Continues

I hitchhiked, which was the preferred way to travel if there was no other means of transport, even during the war. When I reached Uruala, a village on the way, I decided to visit a friend, called Paul, whom Regina and I used to be friendly with. I had met him at a party organised by the Air Force at Uruala, after I had run away from Alex. He had been an officer at the camp who became very interested in me as soon as he saw me. We had exchanged addresses before we left the party and he came to Regina's compound several times to try and see me. Officially, he was not allowed, by tradition, to come in to the compound as girls were forbidden to bring boys home. So he did the usual thing which was to hang around outside till he could get a message in to say he was there. Then the girl would make up a story in order to go out and meet the boy in secret. Of course, in my case, I did what I wanted and openly went out to meet him.

We then went to places and got to know each other well. He was always very good to me and left me money so that I didn't have to borrow. Finally he invited me over to his station and I stayed with him for 4 days, at the end of which he proposed marriage. This instantly put me off, I hated the word, and I wished he hadn't mentioned it. It usually spells the end of my relationship with a man and was certainly the case in this instance. However, my tactic is to pretend to be normal and loving until I work out a way of disappearing. Paul was very insistent but the more he persisted the less interested I became in him and I eventually 'disappeared'.

But now I had a use for him again, and when I knocked on his door he was overwhelmingly pleased to see me. But in the same instant he told me that he had just heard on the radio that Owerri had fallen to the Nigerians and that the war was effectively over. I was amazed as I had just gone past Owerri and had avoided going too close as I could see and hear that it was being heavily bombed. Paul told me that he couldn't leave me alone and insisted that I went with him and his friends towards the enemy in order to try and get behind their lines. The logic of this was that the areas already overrun by the Nigerians would be quiet and, being already subjugated, the people would be calm and not likely to be troubled by the soldiers. On the other hand areas beyond the advancing troops would be in turmoil.

Eight of us crammed into Paul's car and we set off towards where we thought we stood the best chance of getting through the enemy lines. It was a dangerous plan and I was nervous having been in conflict with the Nigerians only a few months earlier. We were stopped several times and often had warning shots fired over our car. Newcasters on the portable radio we had brought told of Nigerians making their final push and that Biafrans should urgently make their way home and dispose of anything (uniforms, weapons, passes, etc.) that might identify them as combatants. We saw many of them throwing their guns away and burning their uniforms in order to look like civilians. The ex-Biafran soldiers were very uneasy as they did not know what to expect of the Nigerians, who were nicknamed 'Vandals'. The lucky ones, like Paul, who had cars were better equipped. So we set off, more in hope than purpose.

We were roughly aiming for the towns of Enugu or Okigwe and eventually reached the Imo river which we would have to cross. There was no way of getting over with the car as there wasn't a bridge in the vicinity of where we hit the river which was about 200 yds wide. so we abandoned the vehicle and our group, consisting of 3 girls and 5 men walked along the bank looking for a suitable place to make an attempt at crossing. Eventually we came to a point where the river narrowed and agreed amongst ourselves that this would have to be it. Then we found that most of us couldn't swim so the two men went to try and find a length of rope. They had to go quite a distance to find a village where this was available. Luckily the water supply in this area was mostly provided by wells so there was plenty of available rope once they found a shop.

On returning to the group the men decided who was the best swimmer amongst us. It was one of the men so he had the rope tied round his waist and set off on his perilous trip. We watched anxiously as he struggled with the current, but he finally made it to the other side after about 30 minutes. He had been swept quite far downstream so he'd had to walk back up the river passing the rope round trees close to the bank so as to make the crossing for the rest of us shorter. Both ends were tied to strong trees. Then in turn each of us pulled ourselves across staying close together in case anyone got into difficulties. We all made it and lay for some time recovering and treating our blistered palms.

Now we were virtually on the front line of the Nigerian advance and could see soldiers ahead. We hid in the bush and discussed what we should do next. I was beginning to wonder if we had done the right thing in making this journey but it was too late to change anything. Finally, it was agreed that the women should go out first and make contact with the soldiers who we could hear shouting, "Friends, friends, no more war; war is over." This turned out to be the policy of the Nigerian leader, General Gowon, who wanted to quickly establish peace and come to an amicable solution with the Biafran people in order to avoid prolonged suffering.

We three girls climbed up the bank to the top of a ridge and out on to a main road where two Nigerian soldiers suddenly appeared. I was terrified but we couldn't avoid them and we just stood there as they came towards us.

One of them smiled and said, "Welcome sisters, the war is over. Up the hill is food and transport for you."

Cautiously, we climbed the hill and were met by an extraordinary sight. People were everywhere and loud speakers were calling on them to come and get help, eat and receive assistance with their problems. A reception area had been set up for displaced people and Nigerian army wives were employed in cooking, feeding and helping anyone who needed assistance. On seeing this we ran back to the men, who were still hiding in the bush, to reassure them that there was no danger and that Biafrans appeared to be being treated well. They weren't convinced and told us to go ahead so that no one would connect them with the pretty girls. Then they followed at a distance until we reached the reception area and they could eventually see that there was no danger.

At the reception area we were invited to eat from a variety of dishes (rice, pounded yam, eba, tuwo, and all kinds of meat). All this had been extremely rare in Biafra during the war and we ate enthusiastically. Additionally, money was being dashed liberally and I collected £180. Lorries were provided to take people to various destinations, and no one was allowed to walk away from the reception points. Having eaten our fill we boarded a lorry and it set off—the first stop was the village of Udi where one of our group lived. This man insisted that we all go with him to see his village and meet his family. He was keen to see how his village had managed in this area as it was some time since he had been home. In fact everything was fine—his parents were in good health but had been concerned for their 4 sons during the war. At least one had now come back. The other villagers, who seemed happy, came out to give this man a huge welcome as they thought he had died. We took part in the celebrations which went on all night and, exhausted, slept long into in the morning until we woke and caught another lorry.

The system was very well organised with people joining and being dropped off at various points along the road. At the end of our journey, which was the town of Umuahia where I had joined the Biafran army, there were 3 of our original group left. This was as far as the Nigerian army would take us.

After being dropped off (Paul, another man and me) we wondered how we would get from here to our homes. Anyway, I couldn't go further since the road and bridge had been destroyed in the fighting. As we were contemplating the situation a military Land Rover approached. Paul and the other man, who were still suspicious, despite the events of the last few days, asked me to walk away from them as they were worried that if we were seen together we would be attacked. This was an intelligent idea as if I'd stayed with them it might have attracted trouble. A young pretty girl with Biafrans was a possible conflict situation with certain types of soldiers.

The Land Rover pulled over next to me and a voice commanded, "Hey girl, come here."

I walked towards the vehicle and the Nigerian officer, a major, asked, "Where are you going? Are you with those men?" (He had obviously seen me with them before moving away).

"Yes," I replied, since it was pointless to lie.

"What's your name?" he demanded.

"Irene Oparaji"

I was surprised at his expression on hearing this. He looked puzzled and I wondered if he knew something that might not be good for me.

Then he asked, "Are you related to Ambrose Oparaji or Odu?"

I didn't know what to say. Whatever I said could have been bad for me.

I felt numb and replied, "Yes, that's my senior brother".
Then he said, incredulously, "Are you really Irene Chioma?"
Again, all I could manage was, "Yes," thinking I should know what he was getting at. But he was starting to look familiar.
His face changed and he became excited. He jumped out of the Land Rover, came over to me, hugged and lifted me into the air. I suddenly realised who he was. He was Mr Nda, a neighbour and best friend of Ambrose in Zaria when I had lived there with him on the Nigerian military base. There was another neighbour in Zaria, Mr Christopher, and we had all lived in adjacent houses. Nda and Chris had competed for my affection, each calling me, jokingly, his wife. It had been totally harmless and the warmth of our lives and the memory of the companionship I had experienced during that period will never fade.

Nda asked me how Ambrose was and I had to tell him that I hadn't seen him since the beginning of the war and I was sure he was dead since, if he had been alive, he would have made an effort to contact me. Nda became very sombre and looked close to tears, and I suddenly felt the same at these memories. He promised me that he would do anything he could to help me. He called to Paul and the other man, who had stayed away from me, and told them to come over, which they did. Then he drove us up to his house where we ate and spent the evening telling stories of the old times to his friends. Nda wanted to keep me at his camp and then take me to see my family, but I said I had to go to Paul's village and then I would come back to him after a week.

The next morning he authorised transport to take us to Item, Paul's village. We were given provisions of all kinds and he gave me £500. Including the earlier dash I now had close on £1000, all donated by the Nigerians in the spirit of harmony and reconciliation at the end of the civil war. This was one of General Gowon's ways of restoring goodwill and I have to admit it was very effective.

Nda made me promise to come back to him as soon as possible as he wanted to do everything that my brother would have done to help me. He gave us more money to get us to where we wanted to go. We then set off for Item.

On arrival at Paul's compound the villagers of Item crowded round, astonished to see him. So many people were never seen or heard of again at this time. Entire family members of military age had vanished without trace. I and my brother Emmanuel were the only survivors of the nine children of Jonathan and Grace Opariji.

Paul's parents were very old but overjoyed to see their son whom they had long given up as dead. They assumed that I was his wife. To them we must have seemed close, and they treated me like a daughter. In fact this made it difficult for us to tell them that we weren't even lovers let alone married, so we kept quiet on the subject. In fact Paul had started to talk about marriage again and I had to make the excuse that we didn't have enough money for this. Additionally there was no work for him and, in reality I wasn't interested in marriage to him, especially as I had now met Nda again and felt more for him. After all I had known him since I was 10 when I had had a crush on him.

I couldn't immediately leave Paul's village to carry on the journey to my home as it was becoming risky for single young women to be alone in the countryside due to Nigerian soldiers anxiously looking for wives before they were sent home to the North. Also the bridge over the Imo river had been destroyed which meant that I would have to backtrack in order to find another crossing making my journey even longer. I therefore stayed with Paul's family for a few months. I was comfortable with the arrangement and happy, for the time being, to pretend to be Paul's wife.

Paul himself became resigned to the fact that I was not going to enter into a quick marriage to him and seemed to make the most out of the pretence. I was alright financially having kept most of the money given to me by the Nigerians as part of Gowon's peace plan for Biafra. I had done quite well in this respect since, for obvious reasons, the Nigerian officers had been happy to give most of the cash donations to women rather than men, and the prettier the women the greater the donation. However, I felt obliged to contribute to Paul and his family's costs as they weren't rich. So when the money started running low I had to think about my next move, especially as peace had returned to the countryside and normal life now prevailed.

I really wanted to find the man who had promised to do what my brother Ambrose would have done for me. This was Nda, the major who had met us on our arrival at Umahia at the end of hostilities, and had given me money and help. I kept thinking of him and now I wanted to take my chances and go back to try and resume a life with someone I had known during the happiest period of my life. Nda was much older than me and this was perfect, as I had always liked older men—they are caring and loving, which are things that I had missed in my life from childhood.

I told Paul and his parents that I had a duty to go and find my family now that travel conditions had improved. This was not strictly true but I had to make up a story that sounded believable. I was nearly 16 and people were saying how beautiful I was—I was popular with men and they all wanted to know me, so I developed a strategy to get as much as I could from the situations in which I found myself. As a cover I developed the character of an innocent pretty girl without much intelligence, which the men adored, and fell for, every time. However, underneath was an ambitious, determined young woman whose real character had been forged out of the pain and experiences (good and bad) of her short life.

I was learning fast the various systems behind man/woman relationships. My experiences with men, so far, taught me that they always wanted to get me for themselves. I had no difficulty in getting a man, it was getting rid of them that was my problem. Even if I was with a man others would tried to get me away from him. Because of this I developed a tactic of extreme rudeness in order to dissuade those who did not interest me, but I can become very charming to those whom I choose to be with. I am also very demanding. Because of the lack of love in my childhood I got, and still get, very angry with my partner if he does not show overwhelming love for me. I need his undivided attention. However, I can press all the right buttons to intrigue a man once I have picked my target. Then I will tease him to the point where he doesn't have much control of the situation. From then on I can usually get whatever I want, when I want it. I realise that men will never give any help to any woman without getting what they want so why should I not do the same.

I bade farewell to Paul and his parents, knowing that I would probably never see them again. I really liked Paul but did not want to get involved in a relationship I was not sure of, and in any case I was still young, maybe not by the standards of a Nigerian woman, but by the standards that I was setting for myself. As a cover I told Paul that if he wanted to see me again he should come and visit me in my village, and I left the address with him.

This was really an excuse to politely escape from the current arrangement in order to follow my dreams of further education and eventual success. Paul took me to the bus station in Item and I paid for my fare to Umuahia where Major Nda was stationed. We made our tearful farewells; he looked broken hearted. I got on the bus and didn't look back.

CHAPTER 10

A Tangled Web

When I arrived at Umahia I went to the compound where Nda had lived only to be told that he had been posted to Enugu, about 150 miles to the East. I should have known that things would obviously have changed after such a long passage of time. I had no money left and, as I often did at moments like this, resorted to the tried and tested means of travel in Nigeria—hitchhiking. After walking in the general direction of Enugu for a while a car stopped for me. The driver told me he was going all the way to Enugu so, elated at this, I got into his car and we set off.

During the long journey we talked about many things. I'm a good conversationalist and find that much of my education has been reinforced with information obtained from others. I told him my situation and embellished it quite a bit with things that I thought he would like to hear. As is usual with men he told me he could look after me better than most, but made it sound like a joke; a form of fishing employed by all men who are interested in a pretty, vulnerable young girl. He bought me food along the way and told me about his family. Then he said we should become friends, but we must keep it to ourselves.

When we eventually got to Enugu he said that he would drop me off at the bus station and that he had a meeting to attend further on in Ude, but that he would be returning to Enugu the next day. He added that he could meet me on the following day if I liked. I accepted his offer and we agreed that I would be at the bus station at 5pm. Then he surprised me by giving me £10 which made me very happy. At least I could now eat.

With no idea of where to look for Nda, I went into the bus station and asked the manager if he knew where the new army people were based. He told me he had no idea so I asked him if I could leave my bag which contained my meagre belongings, most important of which were my wooden doll and education books which I had collected during my wanderings. Everywhere I went I added to my collection in order to feed my obsession for advancement through learning.

On the other hand I only had one change of clothing, which I alternately wore and washed as I moved about. When I could do this I would go down to a river and do my laundry with no soap, then I carried the wet clothes on my head till they were dry. I now had some money so I bought some new clothes. I was amazed at how cheap clothes were in the market. I discovered that they were mostly second hand as a result of the comparatively rich Nigerian soldiers' wives buying in the big stores and selling them, worn only once, in the market. The less affluent civilians had to buy where they could.

I asked the bus station manager if he would look after my bag while I walked around to find out how I could locate Nda. The manager asked how long I would I be and I said that I would be back before he went home after I had found my 'brother'. I thought this sounded more acceptable. Then I went into the public toilet and changed into one of my new dresses so that I would look good for Nda. I decided that asking a soldier might produce better results in my search for him and looked around for one. Eventually I spotted an old man in uniform who had a pronounced limp. I went over to him and said, "Excuse me sir, have you heard about the new Battalion which had moved in from Umuahia?"

He immediately replied, "Yes, but they didn't stop here, they went on to Okigkwe".

This was very far from where I was and I really didn't know how I was going to get there, which I told the old man.

He said, "Maybe I can help you, I am married to an Igbo lady and have 2 children. Anyway it's very risky for you to be around here on your own. The soldiers are mad for young girls like you. Anyway, my brother is looking for a wife and I would like you to meet him. He is looking for a small girl like you."

This wasn't exactly what I had in mind but, as I didn't know where to go that night, I replied, "OK"
. He took me to his house where I met his wife, a big lady called Mama Sunday—she was very nice and welcomed me warmly. She asked me how

I had met her husband, who was called Baba Ijebu, and told me how happy they were together. It turned out that she was of my tribe and had got lost during the fall of Enugu. Baba Ijebu had found her and promised to take care of her. This care ended up with her becoming pregnant. Her parents did not know of her whereabouts so she just stayed where she was with Baba.

Then, when she heard that he had suggested that I meet his brother she said, "Don't do that—he is an air force officer and married with 3 children. He is not the type for you."

I remembered that, when I was walking with Baba to his house, men were whistling and calling to him, "Hey, Baba, Baba, see you later."

I learnt later that this was a reference to the fact that Mama Sunday had a meeting place in her home where she sold shots of liquor to men who came to chat in the evenings. Obviously the men noticed me walking with Baba and thought they would try their hand with me that evening. Later that day the men started arriving at the house and I helped Mama Sunday to serve them. They were very forward with me all trying to introduce themselves, but Mama warned me that they were all married and hopeless and that I shouldn't have anything to do with any of them. However, she told me that there was one man who lived next door, and who doesn't get mixed up with these people. He is responsible for the provision of all the camp food and is someone you should meet. His name is Samuel.

Mama went out briefly and sometime after she came back a man entered the room. She indicated to me, nodding towards him. He definitely stood out from the rest, handsome, and polished. He glanced at me, and when our eyes met I felt a connection with him. He had an immediate effect on me and I wanted to know him. He sat down and ordered his drink without appearing to have much interest in me.

As the night wore on the other customers realised that I was not interested in them and they began to leave. Samuel, who had been drinking on his own, slowly started to engage me in conversation as I brought over his orders. He asked me politely a few mundane questions and then casually suggested that I might like to come over to his place.

I said, "Yes," trying not to seem excited and, after he had left, told Mama Sunday what had happened.

She said, "Good, you should go, he is very nice."

She told me where to go and after I had helped her close up I went over to Samuel's house.

An interesting point to make here is that I had no melting feelings of helplessness that I have heard girls often experience when confronted with a 'man of their dreams'. My life to this point had been hard and unyielding, and whether that is the reason for my lack of emotion, or whether it is because I am put together differently, I don't know. My aim in life is to get out of it what I can, and with men it is no different. My experiences of men are that they usually take what they can from women and often have difficulty in responding or coping with love. I, on the other hand, can see the commercial side and can take from men what I want.

This does not mean, 'I don't know what love is', but rather, 'What can I gain from it?' In fact I have no time for younger men who usually perform as peacocks. I am much more attracted to older, mature men who are more experienced in giving real attention to women. For this reason I do not seem to go through the helpless stage when meeting someone with 'magnetic attraction'. The probable reason for this is because the only real love I had was from my two grandfathers and, fleetingly, from my father. All my contacts with younger men have been uncomfortable and unsatisfactory, at best, or painful and abusive, in the worst cases.

I knocked on Samuel's door and it opened. His relaxed air in Mama Sunday's parlour was now replaced with a more excited look which is the effect that I knew I had on men. He invited me in and I was impressed with the style of his house. We sat down in his lounge and he asked me about myself, sympathising with me in the problems of my journey to find Nda, who by now was becoming a distant memory. Samuel treated me very correctly and eventually worked his way round to telling me that if I wanted he would be happy to assist me in my ambitions. He had cooked us a nice dinner and I asked him about his girlfriends, to which he replied that he did not have one, but that he would love me to be his girlfriend.

After the dinner I went back to Mama Sunday to tell her about my visit and our discussions and she was very happy. I also told her I was going to stay in his house that night. When Baba Ijebu heard this he wasn't happy with that idea, but this was because he wanted to introduce me to his brother. Mama Sunday scolded him and afterwards told me that she wanted the best for me because I was from her tribe.

I then went back to Samuel's house where we carried on with our talk. I told him that I wanted to go back to furthering my education and he responded by saying he would do what he could to get me into a school. In fact General Gowon, the victorious Nigerian President, had issued an order that all children of school age in the Biafran sector would receive 2 years free education, in order to catch up with what they had missed during the war.

I also told him that my things were at the bus station and that I would like to pick them up the next day. He looked a bit worried at this and said, half-jokingly, that I might not come back. He explained that he couldn't take me to the bus station as he had to work. He pleaded with me, slightly self mockingly, to come back and I promised that I would.

Of course, it was inevitable that we would finish up in bed—even Samuel was human. However I was not the total innocent he thought I was and put into practice the old buff trick to avoid intercourse. I went into his bathroom, took a blade from his razor and cut myself. Splashing some blood on toilet paper I simulated my period which Samuel accepted without question, although he did look just a bit disappointed. I didn't really like having to apply this technique but it worked.

Over my early years I had come to learn that men are just big flies. They are all over the place searching for whatever they can get their legs on; they may not always like it but they will taste and test it out. That was my conclusion and I had to charge them, first for tasting, and bad luck for them if they didn't like it. But if they do like it I can allow them some consideration afterwards, but not before. When I was a teenager I always tried to carry my cotton wool and razor blade with me. The reason for this was that I never knew when the darkness would strike. As in the case of Samuel who, without this technique, would have gone the whole way.

This gives me the chance to know the person well and to get as much out of them as I could before giving myself fully which, after all, is what they are after. For, having messed with the woman they will fly away, avoiding her as much as possible. However, if you find a man who is interested in love making, and not just sex, he will do his best to prove it. It was clear that Samuel wanted to keep me otherwise he wouldn't have given me the keys to his house the next day. For me that was love at first sight, because the eyes will eat before the mouth.

Samuel asked me how long it had been, and I told him it had just started and that was why I had had to use his tissue. Nevertheless we enjoyed ourselves with petting and kissing, and, although I felt excitement, I was in full control. We then slept. Before I dropped off I felt the comfortable aura of another impending stage of security about to commence.

So I found love with Samuel and forgot Major Nda. Of course the overriding condition for giving my love was that I should continue with my education and my aim to go to university which is what my father would have wished for me; that was something I had to work on Samuel to get. I knew I was clever enough to get to that level as I was always a bright student but very naughty and able to get away with a lot. I was often punished but it didn't affect my progress as I always read and made up for what I had missed, and still came top of the class. During my various periods of unconnected education I was unfair to my classmates, often leading them astray to the extent that they fell behind. But I secretly worked to catch up myself, which mystified them. I knew that it didn't really matter to them as they mostly came from rich families and would get on in life whatever happened. I didn't have the advantage of that kind of luxury so I drove myself on by burning the candle at both ends.

The next day Samuel gave me £50 to take a cab to the bus station. He also gave me the spare keys to his house which was very trusting of him, and also very risky. But this was the effect that I seemed to have on men. I walked as it was not far. When I got there the station master was very angry saying that I had left my goods for him to look after while I went searching for men. I told him what had happened and he said I should pay him £1 for storage, which I did happily. However, a boy standing nearby, who saw him take the £1, and told him that it was not right to take any money from me. The boy ran after me and gave me £1 of his own.

I refused to take it, saying, "I gave the station master the £1, not you, so please don't worry."

But he insisted so I took it, which made him very happy, and I thanked him for his kindness. There are many instances of civilised behaviour like this which make me very proud of my country.

I then went to the market and bought pomade (makeup), new clothes, panties, dresses, shoes, earrings, etc. All the little luxuries I had missed as a young girl. I made sure that I bought sexy items to keep Samuel happy. This introduced the reality of excitement which in the past I was vaguely aware of, and I was now looking forward to teasing my man. I also bought some things for Mama Sunday and her son Sunday.

Now that I was living in Samuel's house and dressing very sexily, the other officers on the camp were noticing me and becoming jealous of him. Especially the Commanding Officer, who began to arrange for Samuel to be sent away on jobs. On one occasion, when Samuel was away, the CO came to the house. There was a loud knock and, when I opened the door, there he was in his full uniform with his stick under his arm.

He barked out, "Where is Samuel?"

Knowing that he knew perfectly well where he was, I replied as politely as I could, "He's gone to work, sir."

He deflected the logic of this by asking me, "What are you doing here?"

To which I answered, "What do you mean, I'm his fiancé."

The CO persisted, "Would you like me to keep him away from you? I can put you in a hotel, you know."

I said, "No, I don't like that idea, I'm happy where I am."

That made him angry and he snapped, "We'll see about that."

He turned and strode away.

When Samuel came back I told him what had happened. He said that he knew what they were trying to do and, if he didn't move fast, he would be in big trouble. He said the sooner he got me into a school the better. This was easy as General Gowon's 2 year free education programme covered me and all we had to do was find a place. In actual fact only 8 months later the programme was cancelled, but future events in my life would take care of that problem.

The next morning he went to the CCA (Central Commercial Academy) and got me in, subject to tests. He came back looking very pleased and told me what he had arranged. The following week I went for the tests, which I passed easily and then we went shopping for my uniform and beverages, (tea, milk, sugar, Ovaltine, etc.).

I lived in the dormitory during the week and returned to Samuel on Friday for the weekend. This was very successful as I was not so noticeable on the camp at the weekends, and nobody knew where I was during the week. Of course my wild nature was still there, just below the surface, and in moments of boredom during the week I would sneak out at night with my friends to go dancing. This was not allowed so we paid the gateman 10 shillings to let us out and in again early in the morning. On those occasions we only got 1 or 2 hours sleep. Of course Samuel didn't know about this and I was really flirting with danger, especially as I met many boys on these nocturnal outings.

I was very happy with this arrangement as I was doing what I really wanted—furthering my education. Samuel and I became very good friends as we enjoyed each other's company. Eventually he told me that his leave period was due and he wanted to visit his family in his hometown of Jos and, if I wanted, I could come with him to meet them. I agreed to go but actually I tried to think of a way of avoiding the trip as I wasn't ready for any major developments, such as marriage.

When Samuel's leave date came round I told him that I couldn't go because important exams were taking place at the same time and it would be a waste of all my lessons if I missed them. Being a gentleman he accepted this and arranged to go on his own. He gave me £500 pocket money and told me that if I ran short I should go to his friend for anything I needed.

I went to the bus station to see him off. He told me to be a good girl and he would see me in Jos in 3 weeks after my exams were over. I had agreed to do this, but what he didn't know was that I was not going to make that trip either.

After he had gone I went to the market next to the bus station to buy some of my favourite body cream (Monica Smart) with some of the money Samuel had left me. This was just after his bus had driven off. I went into the cosmetics shop, a big expensive store, and as I was walking to the counter I noticed a foreign looking, well-dressed man, looking at me, in fact I recognised him as one the men who had visited the night dances and remembered that I had quite fancied him then. I bought my cream and left the shop to go to another, further down the road. Suddenly I saw the same man behind me—he had followed me, and was now starting to chat me up. He said that anything I wanted I could have and he would pay for it. I didn't believe him at first but went along with it by choosing several expensive dresses. To my surprise he paid for them all.

We started talking, and he invited me to lunch at the market. He asked me about myself and I told him about my schooling and that I had a boyfriend, which he didn't believe because, as he said, a true boyfriend would not leave me to wander about town. We spent the afternoon and evening together and I learnt that he was called Callice by his friends but his real name was Aminu. I also learned that he was actually the owner of the shop in which we had met. He tried to get the name of my boyfriend out of me but I wouldn't tell him. Then he drove me to my dormitory which he wasn't allowed to enter. So we said goodbye in his car, and he told me he would come back to pick me up on Friday so we could spend the weekend at his house.

On Friday he arrived and I brought my belongings down in preparation for the weekend. He drove me to his house which was a bungalow where we enjoyed a very relaxed couple of days.

I liked Callice very much and he was probably the first man for whom I really felt true feelings. The fact that he was not a soldier definitely helped, as I had grown tired of the military attitude, especially towards women. In fact in Biafra at that time it was difficult to find eligible men who were not in uniform. I was extremely comfortable in Callice's company and had decided that he was the man I wanted, not Samuel.

My main problem now was how to handle Samuel. I didn't know what to do as I had promised to join him in Jos. Three weeks passed and I wrote a letter to him explaining that I would not be coming as I was not feeling well enough to travel. However, he responded to this by returning early from his leave to find out the extent of my illness. He was about to find out that he had lost me, for I was now in love with Callice.

All my life was now involved with Callice and I had no time for anyone else. Additionally I had missed a period and this added to the complications of the situation. I told Callice and he was very excited, but I wanted to abort and tried washing it out, which didn't work. In any case Callice would not hear of the termination of his child.

Samuel arrived in the middle of this development and immediately came over to the school to find out how I was. He spoke to the gateman who came to find me and tell me I had a visitor. I sneaked out, against the rules, thinking the visitor was Callice. When I got to the gate I saw, to my horror, the army Landrover and knew it was Samuel. He greeted me and said he had come back specially to see how I was. After leaving some presents he had brought me, he left saying he would pick me up at the gate on Friday as usual.

I now had to work out how to avoid Callice on Friday. I did this by pretending to be ill on Friday morning and being taken to the hospital. In fact I went to see Callice to tell him that the school was going on a trip at the weekend and I would not be able to see him. This gave me a week to try and sort Samuel out. On Friday evening Samuel arrived to collect me and we went off together to his house on the camp.

I had a women friend, called Susan, on the camp. She was an Igbo girl married to a Muslim and I often confided in her. I had told her about Callice and how much I loved him, and had shown her pictures of us together. Of course she also knew about Samuel as she lived on the camp and her husband was a friend of his.

What I hadn't known was that Samuel had visited Susan's husband when he had arrived back from Jos. During this visit Susan had told him that I had been seeing another man and that I had shown her photos of me with him. She also told him that I had said I was in love with this man. When I had shown Susan the photos she had asked me how I could hide them from Samuel. I said that he never looked through my bags or belongings.

When Samuel had collected me on Friday I thought everything was ok, but I detected a change in his manner which I thought was annoyance on his part for me not joining him on his leave. On Saturday night, when we normally went out, he told me we should stay in. We talked about various things, such as how his parents were looking forward to meeting me, and why I hadn't travelled to Jos as planned, especially as I didn't appear to be sick.

He had given me some strong drink, which I thought was unusual as he knew I had a low resistance to alcohol, and after a while I became intoxicated and fell asleep. It was then that Samuel must have gone through my bag and found the photos of Callice and me. He took the photos and hid them, woke me up and said we should go to bed. All night he kept pushing me away from him and I was puzzled thinking that his manner was still due to the fact that I had not joined him in Jos. I had no idea that he knew all about Callice.

The next morning I woke to find he was already up and people from the camp were arriving at the house. They seemed puzzled and uncertain as to why they had been invited. In all, 6 men came, including Susan's husband. Samuel made an announcement which started with an introduction.

Then he proceeded to say, "You should ask Chioma if she is here for me, or is she here for someone else?"

The assembled guests turned to me and one asked, "Well, who are you here for?"

I pretended to be very angry and shouted, "Why is he telling you to ask me such a thing? If he wants to know the answer he should ask me himself. If he has a question for me he should ask this himself."

Samuel immediately stood up and left the room. He returned with the photographs and passed them around. When they had been circulated I snatched one of them from one man and tore it up. Samuel became very agitated, and came across the room to me and started to beat me on my face and legs before anyone else could move. The attack was so violent that I fell down and lost consciousness. The next thing I knew was waking up on the floor with the guests trying to resuscitate me. As I came round Samuel started shouting in my face that I should tell him all about the other man. I didn't speak and the others had to restrain him from attacking me again. They told him not to hit me again, but he was not listening, continuing to demand that I told them about my cheating activities. Then the others started to leave and when I was left alone with Samuel he grabbed me by the cheek, shook me, pulled my ears, and commenced beating me again.

"Stop, Stop," I shouted, trying to cover my head and body at the same time.

But, blind and deaf with rage, he continued, flailing his arms around in a mad fury.

Eventually he paused and snarled, "Right, get out of my house and go back to your bloody friend, whoever he is."

Some neighbours, who had not been present when all this started, had come into the house on hearing the disturbance and attempted to help me get away. They were trying to hold back Samuel who was following me and aiming punches at the back of my head. One neighbour took me to her house and I waited there until I saw Samuel go out to the mess hall. Then I borrowed £5 and quickly ran out of the camp to the bus stop. Luckily a bus was just leaving so I jumped on and rode into town, getting off at the flat Samuel had rented for me, so I could change my clothes. While I was doing this I looked out of the window and saw an army Landrover drawing up outside the house. I told the lady of the house to say she had not seen me and locked myself in the outside toilet. Meanwhile Samuel came in and spoke to the lady who told him nothing, so he went back outside and drove off.

I came out of the toilet and the lady told me that Samuel had gone and it would be better to go somewhere else, rather than wait in her house, in case he came back. He had told her what I had done to him and, since she knew about Callice, I was lucky she hadn't taken his side, especially as he was paying her for my room. She had seen the marks on me and probably didn't want to get involved.

I got some money I had left with this lady and went to Callice's house. Needless to say he was astonished to see me in this state and I told him the whole story. Being the man he was he understood my predicament and, in any case, I was pregnant with his child. He comforted me and I stayed with him in his house that night.

On Monday morning we were woken by banging on the door. It was one of Callice's workers who had brought the shattering news that his shop in town had been burnt down during the night. We assumed that Susan had told Samuel that my boyfriend was the owner of the shop and he had taken his revenge. There was nothing Callice could do as the townspeople were frightened of the soldiers from the camp.

Callice was now in fear of his life and decided that his only option was to flee. In fact he acted so quickly that he left me the next morning while I was still asleep in bed. He was in a hurry as he was convinced that the soldiers would maim or kill him if they found him. He left £1500 on the table with a note telling me he'd gone, but no indication of where to. My immediate thought was that he'd gone to his home country, Cameroon, and I didn't see him for another 6 months.

CHAPTER 11

From Joy into Despair

For a short time I lived in Callice's house with his cousin, who was the houseboy, but I was warned by Callice's workers that Samuel was still out to get his revenge on me so I moved out to live with my Auntie Easter, my father's younger sister, at Enugu. She was shocked to see the state I was in and her first words were, "Thanks be to God, that He loves you". She took me away to her friend's house that same day. My Auntie said it would be safer to rent a different place rather than staying with friends or going back to Callice's bungalow. I had a reasonable amount of money as Callice's workers had brought the last days takings of £3,700 from the shop before it had been destroyed.

So I rented a place and my Auntie got some things together for me to be reasonably comfortable. Patiently, I thought to myself that life must continue, but I was not prepared to have the baby and tried everything to end the pregnancy. This was all to no avail, so I resigned myself to the inevitable, even though I was very sick. One thing I had managed to do was get a testimonial from the principal of my school certifying my education level so that I could continue studying if, and when, I could resume. In order to get this certificate I lied, telling the principal that my brother had moved to Lagos and I was going to move there to join him. Without this story I probably would not have got my testimonial, as the 2 years of free education had been cancelled by the government in the North.

One day the houseboy came to tell me that he had received a message for me from Callice saying that he was living in Port Harcourt. He wrote that, if I had enough money, I should go there but that I should not tell anyone what I was doing. I was overjoyed as I was starting to think that he might be dead, and I immediately started packing my things in readiness for the journey.

It was June 1971, I was 16 and 4 months into my first pregnancy. I set off excitedly to meet the man I had begun to think was gone forever. The bus took about 4 hours and when I finally arrived I followed his instructions to go to the meeting place he had described in his note. When I got there he was nowhere to be seen and I panicked thinking I had missed him. Nevertheless I had enough money to go to a hotel if necessary. Luckily I met someone who knew him and he told me that Callice had a shop and he could take me there.

When I arrived at the shop, there he was, looking exactly the same as I had remembered, and looking very happy to see me. I cried in my relief to see him, and he did too. We became very emotional for a while and cleared the feeling with a 10 minute kiss and hugs. He said he was very happy to see that I had kept the baby and immediately took me to his house where he made me very comfortable, with much pampering and a servant to look after me.

Aged 17, and 5 Months pregnant with
my first child (Chinedu) from Callice.

Callice was my dream man and when I had first met him it was the dream come true. He had everything I wanted. He was 12 years older than me, which was perfect, because I had no intention of marrying a man less than that age difference. He was very sensible, and, after the trouble which I had caused him, had gone away without telling me where and started up a new business which was doing very well. Then after 4 months he had called for me. He had rented a 3 bedroom flat and made it up for me exactly as I had told him I liked my house to be—he had remembered this. I do not think that anyone in this world could have done better. He had placed me where I ought to have been from birth, if death had not intervened. I was the only girl among 9 boys from a very rich family, but I was left with no parents and all the boys except one had died prematurely. But when Callice found me he had wiped away my everlasting tears and did his best to keep me happy. Over the years I had tried to avoid things that I disliked in order to be as happy as possible. Now we decided to get married without the knowledge of the family from which I had become estranged.

Being a Muslim Callice wanted to take me to his home to experience his customs, and I said I would go, but I also said I would not want him near my family, because there was only one true survivor and that was my brother, Emmanuel, who was still a young boy. My other relatives didn't matter and I didn't like most of them anyway. I wanted Emmanuel to be old enough to be married himself before I took my husband home. In this way any dowry paid for me would be available to buy a wife for him, which was the Igbo custom. Anyway, as usual I worked to my own plans ignoring customs and tradition which was my way of getting the best I could out of life.

Officially Callice and I never married, we just called ourselves man and wife which I was happiest with. This worked out fine until the birth of my first child drew near. Callice was very concerned that I had the best medical attention and started enquiring about what we should do as neither of us had any experience or knowledge of this, and we had no family elders of our own to advise us. We were ignorant about the procedure and any problems that we might encounter. A man came to the shop one day and said that he recognised me. He said he was from my area, Mbaise, and told me that my Uncle Chilaka, who was a carpenter, lived in Aba and, if we liked, he would take us to see him. He said it would take about 45 minutes and Callice said we could go in our car with him so he could show us where my uncle lived.

We set off the next day and when we arrived Uncle Chilaka was very surprised to see me. He and his wife were the first of any of my family that I had seen since the war had ended. Callice introduced himself and got on very well with my uncle. We asked them if they could advise us of any way we could get help with the impending birth since as they had children of their own. They told us there was a good German hospital in Aba and Callice was pleased to hear this. He said we should register me at the hospital and, if it was expensive, we should not worry about the cost. We then drove back to Port Harcourt to await my baby's birth which was estimated to be in about 8 days.

Three days later we took all our stuff in preparation for the birth to Aba and I stayed with my uncle and his wife. Two days after this I went into labour. Callice had left money with me so that I could get a message to him when I started. He immediately travelled to Aba on hearing the news and stayed at a hotel. My uncle's house was too small to take us all.

There had been some doubt about how long I had been pregnant. The doctors were not sure because I wasn't very large, but I had told them that I was sure it was 9 months. In the end I went into labour very close to my estimate (15th February 1972) and to everyone's surprise I produced twins. The first arrived, a healthy girl, after 6 hours, but 45 minutes later the second came out stillborn. I was pleased that I had a baby and that I was alright, but sad for the little dead one, another girl. Callice, who had been waiting next door listening to my cries during labour, came in, kissed me and the baby girl, then looked sadly at the dead child. The problem now was that, as I was only 17, my breasts were not developed enough to enable me to feed my daughter naturally. The nurses tried to get me to feed her but it was unsuccessful and eventually we stopped trying. She was given water by spoon and then milk by bottle. I stayed in hospital for a week and then went to my uncle for a day. My uncle's wife was sick and couldn't help much, and Callice was not happy with the condition of the house. So we drove back to Port Harcourt where it was more comfortable for bringing up my baby, who we named Chinedu (meaning 'God is my leader'). That was my name for her, Callice called her Gloria.

Four months later I was pregnant again and this time I benefitted from the experience gained from the first occasion. Callice paid for a maid (also called Gloria) to help me with Chinedu and to do the housework. That made this pregnancy easier than the first.

As my daughter was growing fast Callice's mother invited us to go to Cameroon so she could see her granddaughter. Unbeknown to me this was to become the biggest tragedy of my life. However, we decided to go soon as we did not want to make the trip later than 5 months into my pregnancy. Therefore a few weeks later we drove to the main port to get a boat to Cameroon. The journey was very pleasant and I arrived at Callice's home town feeling relaxed and happy. Chinedu was very good and everything was working out well.

When we got to Callice's mother's house she appeared very welcoming and excited to see us. All the villagers came out to see Callice, his woman and daughter, since his family was very high ranking in the neighbourhood. There was much celebration, singing and dancing. At one point Callice's mother took him and me aside and asked us to come and meet someone. We went to another house and were introduced to a girl some years older than myself, but I was not given a reason for this strange occurrence, which was totally out of the context of the occasion. The girl did not say much and Callice's mother and I returned to the others after a short while.

We were physically very comfortable staying with Callice's family, but after a few days I began to look forward to our return to Nigeria. There was something slightly strange about the atmosphere, especially when we were in the company of Callice's immediate family. I had also begun to notice that the girl to whom we had been introduced at the welcoming party made appearances at times and was looking very sullen and withdrawn. I still wasn't exactly sure who she was but gradually it dawned on me, when I remembered that Callice had told me back in Port Harcourt, in a joking manner, that his family were arranging a marriage for him. He had then set my fears at rest by saying he did not believe in this custom and I had put it out of my mind. Now it came as a shock to me to find that this probability was very real, especially when I learnt that she was sleeping alone in Callice's room where they were eventually supposed to live together. The room that Callice and I shared had been hastily arranged after we had arrived.

An argument between Callice and his mother broke out one day—I couldn't understand what it was about but later his mother approached me and started to explain, as well as she could, that the girl was his first wife by tradition. The wedding ceremony had taken place in Callice's absence, which had made him angry, and was the reason he had not spoken to me about it before we came to Cameroon. He had brought me home to reinforce to his family the fact that I was his first wife. The only problem with this was that we were not married.

This was not his fault as I had delayed any marriage plans until I could make contact with members of my family with whom I had had no contact since the war. It was necessary for me to go through the dowry system and this required the involvement of my family. The situation with Callice was extremely complicated as this girl (from a nearby village and now recognised as Callice's first wife) had been the subject of a longstanding arrangement. In addition Callice's family had paid the dowry to the girl's family and she was already living with them in anticipation of his return. I, on the other hand, was only Callice's fiancé although I had borne him his children. This meant that I would be his second wife, if we married.

In actual fact I wasn't too worried about all this as Callice had already told me something about it and, in any case, I knew he loved only me, I had his children, and we weren't going to live in Cameroon. We were only intending to stay for two weeks.

After about a week four of Callice's friends came to see him, and they all went out. He came back after 3 hours looking very unwell and saying that he wanted to vomit. He asked me to get a bowl but, despite his efforts, nothing came up. I called his mother to tell her he was sick and asked Callice if we should get a doctor. He refused to see anyone then asked me where his watch was and I told him he was wearing it. Then he asked me what the time was and told me to take his watch off. Then he asked for his wallet which I found and gave to him.

He said, "You keep it. You will be alright, sweetheart."

I was suddenly gripped by a cold sweat and I told him to stop frightening me. Then he fell asleep after saying he would be coming back.

His mother then said, "Leave him, he will be alright when he wakes up."

He never woke up. I was lying beside him for some hours when I suddenly felt worried and tried to push him. His body felt very heavy and I went into shock. I cried out for his mother and she came in to the room, looked at him and immediately went out to get help from the neighbours. They came in and said they had called a doctor who eventually came and arranged for Callice to be taken to the hospital, where he was pronounced dead.

It is a horrible memory and I try not to remember the events of that night but it returns at intervals. Our daughter had been sleeping between us when he died and she was the only person I could now trust.

I now felt I was going mad and had strange hallucinations in which Callice appeared at my bedside to give me instructions such as, what to do with his money, and how to get home. While I was lying on the bed he would appear and draw 2 circles on the floor, stand in one and ask me to stand in the other. I would quickly get up to go to my circle but he would disappear before I could get to it. I would hear his voice sometimes and he told me how he had seen a black dot in his drink but still drank it and started to feel sick. He said he was so sorry he had gone out to drink without me.

Unbelievably I stayed about a month in Callice's mother's house after his funeral, unable to work out what I should do. His mother was not much help as she was overcome with the same numbing grief. I was living through a nightmare where the daylight had turned to darkness in a foreign country. I became confused and started begging God to kill me the same way. When this didn't happen I thought of ways to kill myself. I thought that, if I killed myself in time, I could catch him up and we could be together again.

For me at that time, without Callice, it was the end of my life, anyway. I knew no-one in this country apart from his mother and the girl, Lucy, who was supposed to be his wife. The situation was desperate. Here was a man I loved who had brought his young 'wife' to his home in order to show his parents their granddaughter, and tell them that there was another on the way. In the event he lasted only one week and 4 days before dying. It turned out that the four 'friends' who had taken Callice out that evening were relatives of Lucy and had planned his death, since the embarrassment of a foreigner taking the husband of their sister was too great a dishonour for the family to bear. They had poisoned him during the evening.

A few weeks later an old man came to see me. He was a Nigerian and it turned out that he was from my tribe. He was my saviour and told me that he had come to Cameroon when he was 17. He spoke my language very well which made me feel better as the others all spoke French and very little English. It was he who told me that Callice had been poisoned by Lucy's brothers and he advised me to travel back to Nigeria as soon as possible otherwise 'they' would kill me also—especially if my next child was born in Cameroon. I forgot to ask him where he lived so I could see him again if I had any questions or problems. From this point I stopped eating in my mother-in-law's house and began a starvation diet which wasn't helpful to my condition.

However, a strange thing happened a few days after the old man's visit. I had a dream about Callice where he was telling me to go back to the old man and get details on how to get to Port Harcourt. I told Callice that I didn't know where he lived so he gave me directions, which were perfect, as I found his house without trouble. The man was very surprised to see me, especially when I told him who had directed me. I told him I had no idea how to get home so he suggested a route via Kano.

My memory of the events of our escape from Cameroon is vague as my mind was affected by trauma and Callice's periodic ghostly appearances. I remember that I would have to cross a river from a town called Victoria to a village where I could get a bus to Kano. I had to do this without knowing the geography of the country, 5 months pregnant, and with an 8 months old sick baby, plus a suitcase and large food container. In fact I had no idea where I was, and only wanted to get to Port Harcourt. Unfortunately there was no one in Cameroon interested in travel details to Nigeria and, if I'd thought about it, Kano was not the way to go. I had totally relied on Callice when we had come to Cameroon and hadn't observed place names and routes, which I now regretted. The old man said he was pleased that I had taken his advice, but he was no use for intricate travel details. He had probably been in Cameroon so long that he'd lost any sense of scale or direction.

On the day I was due to leave I went to my mother-in-law (it seemed strange to call her that) to say goodbye to her and her neighbours. They had not been antagonistic towards me but I cannot be sure what they really thought of me. The whole affair had, and still has, a dreamlike quality. But my travails were only just beginning. I had quite a lot of cash from Callice's effects and his mother had given me some more, so immediate money was not a problem. Also I was undecided as to whether I really wanted to go to Port Harcourt as, without Callice, it didn't seem to be the place to go. My life has always been a series of highs and lows, which continues to this day. Just when I've reached my lowest ebb and I feel I can no longer cope, things pick up again. So I thought that I should try and make for my home town. Anyway, I had to get to Nigeria first.

I recall that, ludicrously, Callice's mother's last words to me were to make sure that, when my second child was born, I should give some of his/her bath water to my daughter to drink. This would make the two of them bond. Then we left.

CHAPTER 12

The Journey

I and Chinedu went by bus to a boat terminal. This was an open boat which crossed a river. Then we got on another bus which took us to a railway station. I tried to protect my daughter from the mosquitoes as she was very weak from the illness which, I think, had started with the traumatic effects of her father's demise. It was late when we got to the station, and the last train had left, so I lay on the floor of the waiting room with Chinedu in my arms. I had never in my wildest dreams thought that this was how my marriage would end, but now that I was returning to my country, with one child as my companion and another inside me, I was determined to be strong, despite whatever might happen to us.

In the morning, after sleeping fitfully, I heard a train pull in—I had already paid my fare to Ibadan, which is where someone told me I should go, and boarded early. As I had sufficient money I managed to get first class for us, so we were reasonably comfortable for this stage of the journey which took a day and a night. When we arrived at Ibadan, which at least was in Nigeria (in fact almost the other side of Nigeria), I asked the station staff how I could get to the East from here. They looked at me as though I was mad, and I probably was. They said that I must have got on the wrong train as I was going to have to travel South. They said it would take me another 2 days to get to the East which made me very depressed, especially as my daughter's health was deteriorating. A bus took us to Ijebu-Ode, which took 2 hours, and from there I was going to have to get another bus to Port Harcourt. Throughout this nightmare I only had my little girl for company and, when we arrived in Ijebu-Ode, we had to wait for the connection. No one could tell me how long this would be.

Around this time Nigeria was changing the driving side from the left to the right hand side of the road and there were many horrific accidents during the transitional period. I heard people discussing this and it worried me. This also meant that there were more delays in travelling by road than usual. All this was in addition to my anxiety over Chinedu's sickness. In fact by now she was very ill, so in desperation I decided to temporarily discontinue my attempt to get to Port Harcourt and stay in Ijebu-Ode.

Looking back at this period of my life I was doing some really silly things. My actions now look very haphazard with not much aforethought involved. But, although I was a war veteran, I was still only a child and my experiences in life had not really prepared me for planning and executing extensive inter-country travel arrangements. Most travel I had undertaken up to now had been by using the hitchhiking system which depended upon me knowing where I wanted to get to and the benefactor knowing where he was going. But with a baby and luggage I didn't want to take the risk of relying on unscrupulous characters. It is also extraordinary to now think that I had about £9,000 cash on me which would have made our lives so much more comfortable if it had been used properly. Perhaps I was worried that if people knew I had this much money we would be in danger.

Stranded in Ijebu-Ode bus station I now attempted to sort myself out. I realised that it would be too risky to continue and started to be concerned about the large amount of money I was carrying, so I separated out £200 pounds and secured the bulk of it in my large suitcase. While I was doing this I noticed that my daughter, Chinedu, was looking very bad and appeared to be losing consciousness. I asked some people where the nearest hospital was and was told it was quite a distance away, but that there was a pharmacy nearby. Without thinking I asked some roadside hawkers to look after my luggage while I rushed off in a cab with my daughter to the Olushenwu chemist to get medicine for her. I was feeling very stressed and not thinking clearly while everything went wrong.

When I got to the chemist the attendant couldn't help and suggested that I wait for the doctor, who owned the shop, to look at Chinedu. When the doctor came in and looked at her he was shocked and said that she was dying, and if we didn't get her quickly to hospital it would be too late. The doctor drove us himself and when we arrived we were rushed into casualty where she was given oxygen while waiting for a bed in the children's ward. When they moved her into bed she was hooked up to two drips by the nurses, which I was told would cost me a lot, but it was the only solution and I had to rely on the advice at hand. The nurses were very unpleasant to me and told me that my daughter's illness was my fault. They said that she was too young for me to be giving birth to another child so soon after the first, and that was the reason she was so sick. They were quite abusive but I didn't worry about that as long as they helped her. Finally, a doctor came in and ordered the nurses to put her on a respirator.

Chinedu quickly started to respond to the treatment, but the nurses made me sit by the bed and keep her hands away from the drip. I was getting anxious about my belongings at the bus station but I was too overawed to ask the nurses if they could look after her while I went for my stuff. I was worried that they would start the abuse again and got so upset that I started crying. They could see I was a 'baby mother' (a term for an underage mother).

Eventually one of the nurses came over and asked me what the matter was. I explained and she said I should go and get my baggage and get back as soon as possible. I was very grateful and hurried away. I got a cab to the Okwunowu bus station and arrived at about 9pm to find all the day people had gone and the night hawkers had started. There was no sign of my luggage (suitcase and food container) and I felt a sinking feeling in my stomach. However, the bus station manager said that I should go back to the hospital while he investigated. So I got a cab back to the hospital, arriving very late. Exhausted, I lay down in a corridor on the cloth I used to carry Chinedu on my back—it was the only possession that I had left.

Early next morning I returned to the bus station hoping that there would be some good news for a change. Needless to say it was as bad as it could get. The girls with whom I had left my bags had disappeared and there was no sign of any of it. Everything, baby equipment, clothes, and of course the money, had gone. I only had £70 left, my daughter was in intensive care, and I was still a long way from home. It wasn't a pretty picture. The bus station manager was very nice but couldn't help.

In despair, I sat down to think of what to do next. But no answers came so I turned my attention back to Chinedu. At least I had her to take my mind off our dismal situation.

The problems deepened within a week and my money soon completely ran out. A woman I had employed to bring me food stopped coming, for I was now deep in debt, and I resorted to begging for food from visitors. This continued for 2 or 3 weeks and I could feel that the hospital authorities were not happy for us to be there for much longer.

One day a police inspector brought in his son who needed a blood transfusion. He was put in the bed next to Chinedu and hooked up for his treatment. He died soon afterwards. My mind is full of these events and sometimes I wish my memory was not so good. Later the same day two doctors on their rounds stopped at my daughter's bed and told me that I had been there too long and I should take my daughter and leave. I broke down and went outside in despair. While sitting on the doorstep a woman came up to me and suggested that I go and ask the Mbaise people to help me. She said that they were a group of people from my district who met to discuss matters relating to their own community.

I took her advice and went to see them after she had given me an address. I spoke to the chairman (an old man called Chilaka) and he said I should go back to my daughter and they would send delegates to investigate my situation. After they had assessed me they collected £18, but I told them I would need much more to pay my debts, including my daughter's blood transfusions. They took the money back and left.

When the doctors next came on their round they told me again to take my baby away as I couldn't pay for the blood. That was the last straw—I got angry and said loudly, "I thought all General Hospitals were the same. Where do you want me to go with a half dead baby? You are sure she is going to die. That's why you are telling me to take her away. Remember, if my baby dies here in the hospital, the Government will bury her, but if she dies on my way home, which is 500 miles from here, what will I do with the corpse?"

I started crying very loudly which startled the doctors, so they went away and returned to say that they would give her treatment on the basis that we were paupers. She was given 4 pints of blood and responded immediately. From that moment she started to call out when the doctors passed and her recovery was assured. The nurses, who were very sympathetic, also started bringing me food, clothes and general supplies, some of it from their own personal effects. I don't know why this change of heart occurred but it restored my faith in human nature.

We had been in the hospital for nearly 3 months and I was getting close to the birth of my next baby. My daughter was discharged and we were given many presents of food, clothes, money etc. and I even had enough to pay off the woman who had supplied me with food at the beginning of my ordeal. Then by chance I again met Chilaka, the Mbaise group Chairman, who had refused to help me with the hospital costs. He said that, after we were discharged from the hospital, I could bring my daughter and we could stay in his house when he went on his night security work. I was grateful to him for this as I didn't know what I was going to do, now that we were on the road again. I certainly didn't have enough money to resume the journey to Port Harcourt.

On the day we left the hospital the staff crowded round us. We had become very popular after the initial coldness shown to us. I had entered Chinedu into a hospital draw and she had won a prize of £25 and baby milk to last her for 6 months. We also received donations from various people, staff and visitors to the hospital, and the management gave me a card which entitled me to get free treatment when I went into labour with my second child. The matron advised me not to travel in my condition so, with all this kindness, I felt content to stay on in Ijebu-Ode for the impending birth, especially as Chilaka had offered me accommodation.

Two days later I went to register myself with a maternity home and found that the woman manager was the wife of the doctor who had originally taken me to the hospital from the pharmacy. She had heard my story as I was now well known in the town, and after testing my blood said that I needed tablets, which she gave me free. She told me to come back any time I needed anything.

Chinedu and I moved into Chilaka's house shortly afterwards. It was situated in a compound in Ijebu-Ode, but it only had one room so we had to share it with him. He rented this room but, due to the nature of his job, he was out at night, employed permanently on night shift. There were two other occupants in the house, the landlord, who was 105 years old, and a male relative of his who was 95. They had a room each. I slept outside on a mat as I was suffering from the heat, in addition to the pain and worry over my situation.

At this time of year a ceremony takes place surrounding a devil form called the Oro (I know very little about the details as it is forbidden for women to see or know about it). However, I did know that if a women encounters and sees this devil form she will immediately fall asleep and die. For this reason women are not allowed out after midnight during this time.

I was trying to sleep on my mat one evening, when I suspected that my labour was starting. I was aware of the presence of the landlord's son, Shengu, who had just arrived from Lagos. He was telling me that my daughter was crying and I told him that I may have to go into hospital. He asked me which hospital I was registered at, and I told him it was the Oluwushenwu Maternity Home. He offered to escort me there. The time was about 1am in the morning and I was worried about being out at this time, especially as the festival rules forbade it. He told me not to worry as he would ensure that I would be alright.

We had to walk as Shengu didn't have a car, and after about 20 minutes, to my horror, we encountered the Oro procession coming towards us. They were chanting the warning sound, "uuuuuuuuuuuuuuuu" which frightened me and I wanted to go back.

Shengu said, "Don't panic," and removing his babariga (a big loose fitting article of clothing), told me to lie down on the ground and he covered me. He then walked towards the Oro procession and informed the escorts that there was a pregnant woman up ahead who was about to give birth, and he was taking her to hospital.

I lay terrified, crying and praying, on the ground under the babariga and could hear the voices and chanting getting louder as the Oro approached. When they reached me, trembling on the ground, I suddenly felt a hand on my head and heard a voice saying,

"You are going to have a baby boy who will be a very prominent man and give you great joy one day. He will be born very quickly. Get up and go now to the hospital."

This was the Oro speaking and I felt immense calm and relief. I think what saved me was that I did not look up and therefore subconsciously was obeying the rule that no woman should see the apparition. In any case I could hardly move due to stiffness and pain. The others in the procession warned me not to look back and to remember what the Oro had told me.

When they had passed Shengu helped me up and half carried me the remaining ½ mile to the maternity home. When we arrived he knocked on the window and a nurse opened the gate to let us in. They had instructions from the owner, Mrs Oluwushenwu (which means

'Thank God' in the Yoruba dialect of West Nigeria) to let me in whenever I turned up.

I was rushed straight to the maternity ward and the baby was born within 20 minutes on 15th June 1973 at exactly 2:45am. He was a healthy 8lb boy and he was laid on my stomach before the cord was cut. I remembered to request a cup of his first bath water to give to his sister to drink. This had been suggested by Callice's mother as a protection against any detrimental effects from having become pregnant so soon after Chinedu's birth. I was given the cup containing this water and it stood on the table next to my bed until morning.

In the morning when I awoke and my son was brought to me I broke down, remembering that Callice had predicted a boy, and I wished that he had been here to see him. The matron came in and asked why I was sad—I told her I was hungry so she gave a nurse some money to go and buy some food for me. Now I was really concerned about my 13 month old daughter who had been left alone and locked in Chilaka's room and wondered how I could get someone to check on her. Luckily I was visited by a woman I knew, called Nwunugbo who ran a beer parlour at the front of the compound where Chilaka lived. I had helped her with the parlour, serving and cleaning. She had been told where I was and had come to see if I was alright. She had not been to check on Chinedu as I had the key, but she said she had not heard any crying.

I asked to be discharged and was told that if I felt strong enough I could go. I got up, dressed quickly and then asked for the bill. The nurses told me not to worry about it as the matron had delivered me without charge. I was shocked and felt very humble at this kindness. I cried and went to give my thanks to the matron who told me to go home and look after myself. She added that I should go back to them if I ever needed anything.

I left with Nwunugbo carrying my new son whom I called Osinachai (This can be interpreted as "A gift from God", but he came to be known as 'Osi' for short). We got a taxi back to the house and, when we arrived, I couldn't get in to check on Chinedu quickly enough. She had been asleep when I left and, although she was awake when I got home, she was lying quite happily on the mattress. I was so happy to see her again, especially as I had thought I would not survive after my encounter with the Oro. After all the months of pressure I was, at last, with my two children and able to concentrate on the immediate future.

Oddly, at this moment my mind turned to Callice's mother and I recalled that she had asked me on the day I left her house if I would be bringing back her grandchildren to see her one day. She said that I should go back to run Callice's business in Port Harcourt and to write and let her know how I was getting on. She added that she might come over to help me with the children as they will be the only grandchildren she will have. She had then told me about giving Osi's first drop of bathwater to Chinedu to drink, and that she would explain the reason behind that when we next met. To make her happy I had told her I would return but, in reality, all I wanted to do was get away from the country and the wicked people who had killed my true love, the man who had meant everything in this world to me. I never wanted to see anybody from that part of the world again and I have never tried to contact her, even though she had eventually treated me like her own daughter.

I had been very careful with the money that had been given to me by the various good people of Ijebu-Ode Hospital. With this money I was able to buy various necessities for my children and myself. This was fortunate as I was told that travelling on the roads was still risky, so I decided to stay on in Ijebu-Ode for the time being. Chilaka was agreeable to my staying in his room.

However, I was somewhat concerned about his intentions as he had been showing rather too much interest in me before my son was born. I had been able to ward off his advances while I was pregnant but now I would have to be on my guard. His problem was that he had never been married and had thought he might have a chance with me, especially as I needed help. But he was about 70 and the last person I wanted to get involved with. Now that I was returning to normal, he was resuming his attempts to woo me. He was really a good man with his own problems of loneliness and frustration, and had helped me through this complicated period in my life. He had always helped with purchases of food and made sure that I was as comfortable as possible. However, unfortunately I wasn't interested in him, after all he was 70 and I was 18.

As time went on I had to plan how I should finance myself and my children independently, but still I stayed on in Chilaka's room. This confused him as he couldn't work out what my intentions were. I really didn't want to make the journey to Port Harcourt for two reasons. These were the danger in travelling, especially with two small children, and the mental effect on me of returning to Callice's house without him, knowing how happy he would have been with his children. I was basically very mixed up and poor Chilaka was getting increasingly perplexed. He was trying his best to make me happy but I could understand that my presence was disturbing him because he was a man with desires and I was a dream woman who had miraculously entered his dreary life. How could he think otherwise. He was trying to work his way towards a deeper relationship but, in no way, was I going to get into that so I continued to hold him off.

Moreover, my money was running out—I only had £50 left with no prospect of any more coming in, so I started to work out a way of earning an income. If I ran out of finance completely I would be even more vulnerable to Chilaka's advances. I had to devise a means of making cash. I had noticed that the beer parlour in front of Chilaka's house, run by my woman friend Nwunugbo, only served drink, not food. So I struck on the idea of providing nibbles for the drinkers. I discussed this with Nwunugbo and she was agreeable to this, if I could produce something that her customers would like. She had not bothered to provide food herself as it was too much trouble.

I made my mind up to try this and, one morning, I left my children with Chilaka after he had returned from work and went to the meat market. There were individual heaps of goatfoot for sale at £10 per heap so I bought one heap and paid £2 to the butcher to clean and cut them to size. Then I took them home, washed and cooked them, to my special recipe, in the area behind the parlour. (At least my past skill as a servant was about to prove useful).

As I was doing this people around kept coming up and asking what the delicious smell was. One man, a drinker at the parlour, asked for some when I told him what it was, but I said that it wasn't ready yet. So he ordered a plate and went in to drink with his friends. When I brought in his soup all the drinkers started clamouring for some. My entire stock went in a flash—there wasn't enough and many were disappointed having arrived too late. I made £49 that day, which was a profit of £31 after I had bought firewood and vegetables on top of the goatfoot.

Next morning I went very early to the market—as soon as Chilaka had returned from his work. At this time I had a better choice of quality and bought 2 heaps of goatfoot and had them cleaned and cut. I made friends with the stallholders and started to get better deals and quality of meat. This made me £100 (£70 profit) at the beer parlour. Word was now getting round about my soup which was called Nkwo (literally meaning 'I can't stop') and Nwunugbo was getting overwhelmed with customers. She was starting to run out of drink to cover the increase in trade and, as she didn't have enough cash to buy more stock, asked me to give her money to cover this.

Actually I had not been paid for the serving and cleaning work I had done for Nwunugbo during my poor days and I felt I was doing her a favour by increasing her trade. Now she was suggesting that I paid her a rent which I did not think was fair. Jealousy was setting in as she knew that I was now earning more than her. For a month she nagged me about the imbalance of our respective earnings.

Every day she was selling 3 jars of palm wine by midday whereas one jar had previously lasted all day. Palm wine had to be brewed to order and delivered very early in the morning. If it runs out it can't be quickly re-stocked as the trees require to be tapped. Nwunugbo did not have the working capital to keep up with the increased cashflow and continuously demanded that I give her money to cover this. I had already given her £80 and now she was asking for more without repaying anything. Therefore, I decided to ignore her demands and carry on as normal. She then started to become more interested in my kitchen business with the obvious intention of trying to get into it herself. After a while, when it was obvious she wanted to take over my line, I had to decide whether or not to break with her.

During this period Chilaka's interest in me was increasing and he was doing everything he could think of to please me. One Sunday afternoon I cooked lunch for us and left it on the table for Chilaka and me while I breastfed Osi (my breastfeeding skills were much improved from the days of Chinedu's birth). When I returned to my lunch I found it covered in charcoal. Chileka, who had finished his meal, asked if he could help by holding Osi.

I said to him, "What's this on my food, are you trying to kill me?"

He replied, "Don't worry it's nothing bad; eat it, it's only something for love."

I came out into the open, over his obsession with me and said, angrily, "Are you trying to make Ju Ju for me to make love to you."

He looked embarrassed and mumbled, "Why not, it's only for love—there's nothing bad about it."

Furiously, I told him, "That is very, very bad," and threw my food away.

The next day, when Nwunugbo came to the parlour, I told her what had happened. Her response was to ask me why I was being so difficult.

"He only wants you to love him, why don't you accept this?" "He is a kind man and you have been living rent free, why don't you accept him?"

This was not what I wanted to hear. I realised that she did not sympathise with my situation and, at that point, I made up my mind to make the break and move away from both of them completely. I had made quite a bit of money from my goatfoot soup and was not now tied to anyone financially.

I continued to run my food business for a week but relations with Nwunugbo had become very strained. She was unhappy with my attitude and the fact that I did not accept her advice to settle down with Chilaka. Also she was obviously very envious of my success which had been built on her business and local contacts, and now wanted to do something similar herself. As relations had broken down I made the decision to leave as soon as possible and find a place for myself and my children to live. I easily found a room to rent but did not find it so easy to source business premises for my money making activity.

In fact I wasn't able to find a way of carrying on the cooking trade, especially as I had two small children to look after, and now the money was again rapidly running out. This meant I couldn't revert back to my other option, which was to resume the journey to Port Harcourt or my home. Once again I was stranded and I had to find something that enabled me to make some money and be with my children at the same time.

I hit on the idea of offering to teach children using my education skills and languages. This was basically a babysitting service with extras. I spoke to our neighbours around where we were living and got the impression that this was a much needed requirement for the working inhabitants. I was encouraged by this, especially as no certificate or licence was required to set up and run this kind of establishment. With my remaining cash I bought two benches, a blackboard and a box of chalks. I set these up in the garden outside my rented room which, conveniently, was on the ground floor.

I campaigned for clients and managed to take on 10 children for varying periods. Some, for the whole day, and others for a couple of hours. I charged £1 per hour and managed to get by on this, paying the rent, food and clothing for my children. During the dry season this worked well, but when the rains came the garden and my room suddenly flooded up to my knees. I bought bricks and plywood to raise up our bed and keep us and our belongings above the water. This situation lasted for 3 months during which I could not take the children so I had no income of any kind. Eventually I could no longer tolerate this compound and moved us out to a flat on a first floor. This was more expensive than the old room but, at least, it was dry.

In front of this house was a restaurant where working people ate. There was a police station nearby which provided clients. At this point I was penniless and all I could get was dash by begging, However, I asked the lady running the restaurant (she was known as Mama Bose; pronounced Bosey) if I could help by washing, sweeping and cleaning for her. She recognised that I was a hard worker and grew to like me. Now I was feeding myself and my children on the leftovers from the restaurant, but Mama Bose started to give me a bit extra and I began to be able to save a little.

As my children grew it was very noticeable that were very happy in their own company, hardly ever fighting or arguing. They both had the same mannerisms and character, but the big problem was that when Chinedu was sick Osi followed with the same complaint within hours. I wondered about this and why the infections were being passed between them every time they occurred. They recovered in exactly the same way.

Then my children became very sick with whooping cough, measles etc. Mama Bose's husband, Majekodum, who was blind and had been a doctor, took me and the children to a native doctor. This doctor told me that the children would die, one after the other, and on the same day. He based this on the fact that my son was worse in the morning and my daughter got worse in the evening (i.e.following each other). He said that this was caused by something I had done in the past and asked me what this might have been. I told him all I think of was that I had given Chinedu some of Osi's water from his first bath to drink.

I asked the doctor, "How can I stop my children's illnesses."

He said, ominously, "it's going to be a long process involving buying and killing two goats and reserving a plot in the local cemetery."

Aged 19 with Mama Bose (right) in Ijebu-Ode (1974).

He continued by telling me that a ceremony would be held for the goats, requiring coffins, to combat the prediction that both my children would die on the same day. This was going to be expensive and all I could afford were the goats, the plot, white cloth to wrap the goats in, and rope to tie the goats. I bought all this with my last few pounds and the doctor made arrangements for the event to take place the following week.

The ceremony happened as planned with lots of chanting and blood. The goats were killed and dressed up like humans, and then buried. I came away hoping that this would solve my problems and the native doctor assured me that everything would be ok and that nothing further would happen to the children.

However, after one week Osi was seriously sick with whooping cough and a skin complication which spread boils all over his body. His skin eventually became the constituency of chewing gum. I prayed and prayed and questioned God why he'd given me children if this was to happen. Osi's worst periods were at night and I demanded from God the answer to why He made these things happen at times when help was not at hand. Both children were similarly affected, and I was told that they were affected by a combination of measles and chicken-pox, on top of whooping cough.

I was not able to help Mama Bose while this was happening and she was very good about it, sending food up to me. It got to the stage where I started to lose my grip on sanity and I found myself putting the children in the garden and covering them with leaves and rubbish, hoping they would mercifully die. I watched from the window but they kept moving, so I ran down and brought them back in. I prayed that they did not die at night when I had no help. I challenged God to find someone to help me, but no help came. I was too proud and ashamed to go back to begging for free help from the hospital.

This went on for about two weeks and then I suddenly exploded. I shouted to God that if he didn't help I would run away and leave them and kill myself. That was on a Thursday—on the following Sunday night Osi became even worse and I was convinced that he was already dead. I went to another lodger in the house, a man called Bathram, and told him that I had to bury my son. He took it calmly and said he would get a shovel. Then he carried Osi, wrapped in his sleeping cloth, and went down and out on to the road verge. We waited in the darkness for a car to pass, but the car stopped alongside us and the driver, a policeman I had known from the beer parlour, got out and asked us what we were doing.

I told him, "We're going to bury my son because he is dead."

The policeman raised his eyebrows and said, "No, you can't do that, I'll take you to the hospital."

We all got into his car and he drove us very fast without stopping, even for traffic lights. I had the strange feeling that we were driving on the wrong side of the road and, in my confused state, we probably were.

On arrival Osi was carried in and immediately given oxygen which made him cough, and he opened his eyes. They gave him a bed and he was in for 2 weeks with all the attention that he needed, medicine and children's food (Cow & Gate which was difficult to get outside). He recovered well over the next month.

Chinedu had been very ill at the same time but did not go into hospital. When Osi was discharged I brought him back with his medicine and Chinedu miraculously started to improve. I shared the medicine between them and gradually they returned to good health. To this day they are still very close to each other and have never been seriously ill again.

Although I consider myself a Christian I am convinced that the spell cast on them, when Chinedu drank Osi's bathwater, had been broken by the native doctor's goat ceremony.

Now that my children were much stronger I took the job waitressing in Mama Bose's restaurant for £2.50 per month. Including tips and left-over food I was able to feed my children and pay the rent. I was more secure than before because I was now one of the restaurant staff.

CHAPTER 13

On the Move Again

One day a man came into the restaurant with his friends. He was talking to the others in Hausa so I could understand what he was saying. I couldn't restrain myself and said something to him in Hausa. He became very interested in me and said that he had been a soldier but was invalided out after being wounded. We talked for a bit in Hausa and he took my details and then asked if he could write to me from Lagos where he was going. Before he left the restaurant, he came up to me and gave me £20. I was so happy with this and he told me he would write to me as soon as he got to Lagos.

A week later he returned and surprised me by asking if he could sleep in my room that night. I said he could, but he would have to sleep on the floor like the rest of us. The next day he bought a big bed for all of us and stayed for 3 days. After a few months he, Joe, became a frequent visitor and then I realised I was pregnant. He said that it might be better if

I went with him to his home town of Gboko as he didn't like Ijebu-Ode. This suited me as Nguru was on the way so I could drop my children off with my stepmother, Jemima. We made the travel arrangements and I told Mama Bose that I would be leaving. She had suspected that this was going to happen as she could see I was pregnant and in love with Joe.

So we set off and when we reached Nguru I introduced Joe as my fiancé. I gave money to Jemima to cook a big meal for the family and in the evening I told them my story from when they had last seen me, bringing my brother Emmanuel back to the village to recuperate from his wounds, until now, about 3 years. I explained that Osi and Chinedu were the children of my first husband who had died in his home country of Cameroon, and now I was in love with Joe, with whom I would soon have a child. The villagers told me that two men had visited the village at

117

different times asking for me. They had traced me from the address I had given them. These men were Alex and Samuel, both of whom I had run away from due to their violent behavior. The villagers had had no idea of my whereabouts and even thought I might be dead, so they could tell them nothing about me.

In the morning, before my children woke, I left with Joe to go to his village, Gboko. We travelled by car and it took 5 hours. It was late when we arrived and I was immediately introduced to Joe's father, his wife, and his brother. Joe's natural mother had died but his father had re-married. We were given a nice thatched house in the compound and slept happily. In fact I was happier than I'd been for a long time.

The bed was empty beside me when I woke in the morning. Joe had gone and I was upset as I had not been properly introduced to his family in the daylight. It was most embarrassing as they kept asking me where he was, as if I was keeping something from them. I couldn't explain where he was and just had to lamely tell them that I didn't know.

It was late in the evening when he returned, walking in as if nothing had happened.

"Where have you been?" I said, "Why did you leave without explanation, embarrassing me in front of your family whom I hardly know."

Casually, he replied, "There's nothing wrong in that. My friends had not seen me since the war and I couldn't refuse to join them."

I gave him the food that his stepmother had prepared and as he was eating I walked out to our room. I took a torch and looked for the car keys, first in our room, and then in the car. The reason I was doing this was because he had suggested that he might be going off again and I was certainly not going to be left in another embarrassing situation. While I was looking in the car ignition for the keys I was aware that there was someone in the passenger seat. I jumped back in fright and, on looking again, saw it was a woman. In that instant I knew that this relationship was not what I had thought it was.

I snatched the key from the ignition and ran back to the house, with it hidden in my wrapper, and confronted Joe. I asked him why he had brought me to his home only to leave me on the first night.

He erupted, stood up, threw the food on the floor and stalked towards the door shouting,

"Who the hell do you think you are?" And then walked out.

Minutes later he was back, bellowing furiously, "Where's the car key, Where's the key?"

I replied, "Why are you asking me? You drove back here."

He went out again and I heard shouting from the car

The woman in the car was protesting that she did not have the key. "Your wife came over and took it."

There was silence. Then in he burst again demanding the key from me. His face was contorted with fury and I inflamed the situation by refusing to comprehend what he was talking about.

"Give me the key, Give me the key," he kept on repeating.

Then his father, who had heard the commotion, came in and, after seeing the state his son was in, called me out to try and resolve the matter. Joe followed, threatening violence, and his father pleaded with me to give him the key, if I had it. Before I could get the key out of my wrapper Joe lunged at me and started beating me around the head. I couldn't get the key out and fell unconscious on the floor. When I came round I told the stepmother to take the key out of my wrapper and give it to Joe who snatched it and stalked out.

That night I slept in the same room as his father and stepmother in case Joe returned during the night. In fact he turned up the next day, drunk and haggard, and slept all day. In the evening he rose, showered and went out without a word. That incident, so early in our relationship, told me that we were going nowhere together. However the reality was that I was pregnant and therefore I had to devise a plan that suited me in this latest situation of my life.

In the weeks that followed Joe's routine continued much along the same lines. He was around for half the time, often coming home at 2am demanding food which had to be hot. I had to be up waiting for him so I could set the fire and prepare his dinner at short notice. If I didn't perform to his satisfaction I was beaten. Then there were his sexual demands which had to be complied with whenever he wanted it. Eventually I was operating automatically in order to fulfil two objectives, avoiding the beatings and keeping a home for my children.

In fact it was not all bad. Joe's parents were a golden couple who loved me. His father, even gave me my own farm in the hope that I would stay with them, despite his awful son. However, I had decided that I could never stay permanently in this atmosphere, but out of respect for his parents I would remain until their grandson was born.

Time marched on and I went into labour for the third time. I was taken to a maternity home by Joe who, for a change, was quite attentive. A baby boy of 8 lbs was the result and Joseph decided he would be called Nndetive, but I called him Godwin and his Igbo name of Onyenach (Meaning 'We have our individual beliefs'). Joe was very pleased and celebrated with his friends for days. As soon as he decided that he was no longer required to be present he resumed his nightly activities.

After about three weeks Joe came in late, as usual, demanding his rights. This time when I refused to comply an argument ensued, finishing with the first beating I had had for some time. On this occasion his father intervened and managed to stop him with a mixture of cajoling and admonishment. As sometimes happened Joe became sorrowful and apologetic.

He mumbled, incoherently, "I'm sorry, I'm sorry—I won't do it again."

Of course this promise was always short lived and the dreadful act was repeated at regular intervals.

When Godwin was 5 months old I made a trip to Lagos with a lorry load of yams. Godwin was left with his father and my niece, Susan, whom I had brought from Mbaise as help for me before Godwin was born. I sold the yams for a good price—it worked out at £200 profit for the whole operation. On my return I noticed that Susan appeared to be upset and eventually told me that my husband (although we were not married, everyone called us husband and wife, as is the custom where two people are living together) was not a very good person. She said that he had been sleeping in my bed with a woman from the town.

Later, Joe somehow found out that Susan had told me this and started to work himself up into a fury. Eventually he could contain himself no longer and confronted Susan, demanding to know who she thought she was to be spreading malicious lies about him.

Susan tried to get away but he grabbed her and started to beat her in his expert fashion. He really seemed to take pleasure in inflicting pain on those weaker than himself. I heard the her cries from outside and ran into the room to witness Susan being knocked to the floor under a rain of blows. This was too much. I had resigned myself to his attacks on me but this was different as he had no rights over Susan. I was overcome with fury and Joe, who had his back to me as he continued with the attack, did not know what was coming. I quickly tied my skirt up around my waist, came up behind him, clamped my arms around his waist and bit him deeply in the fleshy part of his side. I then swung him from side to side, gaining momentum, before releasing him suddenly so that he flew to the concrete floor cracking and grinding his face in the grit. He sat up and turned to look at me, blood seeping from the lacerations on his face. Then he tried to get up and start on me, but Susan and I were out of the room and away before he could get to his feet. We ran out of the compound and down to the police station in town. However, the police were not too interested in our story, mainly because I was Igbo and Joe's family were of the Tiv tribe. They were reluctant to take action against their brother tribesman.

So we went to a different compound in the village where we knew some local people. It turned out that they knew all about Joe's methods and behaviour towards me and had been disgusted by it for some time. They immediately called a meeting, which included Joe's relatives, in order to discuss the situation. Joe was called to attend and he was made to swear an oath that he would never harm me again. He really looked pathetic with his face scarred and holding his side where I had bitten him. I don't know whether he really understood what the villagers thought of him, or whether he even cared, as he had a very high opinion of himself.

During the period when Susan and I were at the police station Godwin had started crying and wouldn't stop. Joe had tried to calm him, despite his wounds, and had asked other women in his compound to help.

They had refused, saying, "You have got rid of the mother, so you can now look after the child."

When I returned to the house Joe quickly left and didn't return until next morning, drunk as usual, and looking even more terrible from his injuries than he had the previous evening. He spoke to me slightly more deferentially and I felt happier with the situation following the incident and the villagers' meeting. Life continued much as before but Joe still lost control at times and really couldn't get out of the habit of violence which was ingrained in him. Most times he just shouted at me.

The staff of UKPI school in Gboko. I was a primary school teacher (Lying on the ground in front) aged 21.

Now my outlook on life was different as far as my association with Joe was concerned. My pregnancy, which had tied me to him, was in the past and I began to make plans for my future, which did not include him. Joe's father, owned and ran a school (Ukpi Primary School) in Yandave. To try and help me, and knowing I was educated to Standard 6 level, he offered me a teaching position with the promise of training me for higher qualifications. He and his wife were good people and I liked them, but I couldn't stay with Joe; it would have been an impossible situation. However, I accepted the teaching post as a temporary measure.

Despite the fact that Joe's family were loving and kind towards me I could no longer tolerate living with an ignorant, vicious, uncivilised man. I kept these feelings to myself knowing that, before long, I would be gone, and gone for good. He still hit me and forced me to satisfy him when he wanted it, without considering my feelings, but I handled this as best I could. On one occasion he hit me several times. This was as a result of me not putting meat in his soup which I couldn't do as he hadn't given me enough money. He responded by throwing the soup over me and going to bed.

I was very angry at the incredible unfairness of this and lay awake beside him until he was snoring. I watched him and the more I looked at him the more I realised how much I hated him. I quietly got up and went into the kitchen to get some ground pepper. I came back and waited until I was sure he was fast asleep, before sprinkling the pepper over his face and eyes. Then I lay down and pretended to be asleep. Eventually he started to twitch as he breathed in the spice.

Suddenly, he awoke and shrieked, "I can't see, I can't see!" and screamed more loudly as the pain intensified.

I lay quietly pretending to snore, until he shouted my name and I sat up. I tried to look concerned and said, "You must have splashed some of the soup over yourself".

He wasn't listening, just yelling at me to do something to help him.

I got some water and gave it to him to wash his face, but this made it worse so I tried the old Nigerian remedy of giving him salt to lick, which is supposed to suppress eye irritation. This actually helped and he calmed down, so I left him and went to spend the rest of the night on the floor in another room. In the morning I got up, dressed ready for school and left without seeing Joe. After school I returned to the compound, made dinner and fed him and his family. As usual he left after dinner for his evening recreation so I cleaned the house and went to bed with my baby. This routine repeated itself most days with Joe returning at 2 or 3 in the morning, waking me to get his food warmed. I was quite frightened at having to cross from the main house to the kitchen area in the dark. This duty included me having to sit with him while he ate, and then clearing the table while he either slept on the sofa or went to bed.

I was now looking forward to the school holiday period as that was the starting point for my escape plan. When it finally arrived I reminded him that I wanted to see my other children, Osi and Chinedu, whom I had left in Mbaise.

He agreed to this and the night before I was due to leave, asked, "What are you taking with you?"

"I'm taking my box." I answered.

He responded to this by saying, "Why do you need the box if you're only going for 4 days?"

"OK, that's alright, I don't need to go with much so I won't take it." I agreed, in order to keep him relaxed about my trip.

He drove me, Godwin and Susan to the bus station where we said goodbye to him. He appeared happy that we were leaving, presumably because it was freeing him to get on with his fun. In his arrogant way he was oblivious to the fact that I was walking out on him. Susan knew about my plan and we were both happy in the knowledge that we would never be coming back.

CHAPTER 14

Success at Last

When we arrived in Nguru there was a great welcome for us. Osi and Chinedu were overjoyed to see me as I had only visited them once during the year I'd been away. My stepmother, Jemima, asked me when I was going back to Joe and I told her that I might not be going back straight away. I kept it vague so that people would not know what I was going to do next.

This triggered her off and she said smugly, "No man would stay with you. You don't have the right character to keep a man."

This goaded me into responding, "I told you that I wasn't going anywhere until you were dead and your corpse sent back to your parents like my mother's body was sent back to hers."

It was my way of putting her back in her place and it worked, as a flicker of fear crossed her features. All along she had despised me for not wanting a husband. In fact she had read my character from the label I was carrying when I first met her—that of an orphan and devil who should have died at birth. Children who kill their mothers are witches and would normally be burnt anyway. However, in Jemima's mind I could just as easily kill her so she gave up the unequal struggle. I think she really was scared of me.

Anyway, Jemima preferred it when I was away, as I sent her money to look after my children and I knew she didn't use all the money on them. So she was visibly disappointed when I told her that I was taking all my children away to live somewhere else. I didn't give any indication as to where we were going as I didn't want people trying to find me. I knew that previous acquaintances had already been around looking for me and the last thing I wanted was for Joe to turn up. After a few days in Nguru we got our stuff together. There wasn't much as I'd had to leave most of my belongings in Gboko in order to allay Joe's suspicions and give me time to get well clear of him. I had decided to return to Ijebu-Ode where I had good friends and life for my growing family would be reasonably settled.

We left early in the morning and I felt elated as we were all together again, setting out on the next stage of our unpredictable voyage through life. This feeling was short-lived as, when we arrived at Ijebu-Ode, I couldn't find any suitable accommodation and we all had to stay with Mama Bose. This wasn't very satisfactory and she could only take us for a short period. After a few weeks one of Mama Bose's rented rooms in her compound became available and we moved there. However, I wasn't making enough money to cover all my outgoings and I began to run seriously short of money. This was a return to an old condition—penury—which I had forgotten during my period with Joe's family. Things became difficult as the weeks passed and the old desperate feelings of taking the easy way out by killing my children and myself began to re-emerge.

One of my bad times. Only 21 and looking 50.

I was 21 but, when I looked at myself, I saw the reflection of a 50 year old. The recent years had taken their toll on me and every time I seemed to have found security and happiness I was dumped back in another demanding situation. Every night I called to God in my mind and imagined that He was looking at me while I was speaking to Him. I was telling Him exactly how I felt and what I was going to do if He did nothing to help me. When nothing happened, I became enraged and, as I'd done at times like this in the past, I angrily challenged Him by saying, "Why are you ignoring me when I need help? You must provide me with help so that I can support my children. I didn't ask for them, so why did you give them to me if you won't provide for them. Why are rich people wicked and do not extend help to poor people? Why cannot you enable me to make and save £100 with all other needs covered—then you will see that I will feed every ant in my house."

I really feel that God is present in me when I speak to Him on these occasions. It's as if I am making a covenant with Him. At that time I was beginning to view the church and conventional God as convenient instruments invented by so-called Christians to use for their own ends. My interpretation was that God existed as a supreme energy within me, and that any righteous person should act as an individual and not necessarily in accordance with church rules. I had begun to notice that many 'really good people' were not necessarily practicing Christians but ordinary people with real feelings of love and decency towards their fellows. This is what I call 'God in existence through man.'

Following this final confrontation with Him I became aware of a voice saying to me, "This Sunday get up and go with your neighbour to a town meeting."

The voice repeated this many times saying, "Don't forget, you must go with her to the meeting."

On the Sunday I asked Mama Bose to look after my children for two hours and went round to see my neighbour, Geraldine. I told her that I would like to go to a meeting with her (She had often invited me to go in the past). She was pleased that I had at last accepted her offer, but I didn't tell her why I had suddenly decided to do this. We set off for the venue and there were many people arriving as we got there.

After circulating and being introduced to others I noticed a pretty girl, who looked slightly older than me, and summoned up the courage to go across and speak to her. She had interested me because she reminded me of myself in her manner and somehow I felt drawn towards her.

I asked her if I could have a word in private and she replied, "Yes, could you wait a moment?"

She finished her conversation with some other people and then came over to me.

We introduced ourselves. She was called Agnes and told me that she worked for Okenla Tyre Factory, one of the biggest companies in Ijebu-Ode, and that she frequently travelled on business to Lagos. I was interested in the sound of that and asked her straight out if she could help me to find a job anywhere, as long as I could support my children. I was almost tearful as I spoke and she looked touched by my obvious desperation.

She then asked, "But who will look after your children while you're at work?"

I quickly reassured her, "They are with my landlady just now."

But she persisted, "I mean, who would look after them if you had to go away to work without them?"

Hoping I wasn't putting her off, I said, "I can leave them with her but I will have to pay her something from anything I might earn."

To my enormous relief this seemed to satisfy Agnes and she said, almost casually, "I do have a job which might suit you. The work period would be from Friday evening to Monday morning."

She went on to say that she was going to Lagos the following Friday and I could join her if I wanted to. I had to say that I couldn't go as I had very little money, but she told me that she could help me out until I could repay her. She said she was quite sure that my luck would shine, which I didn't understand, but it sounded encouraging. She also said that I should leave whatever money I had with whoever was looking after my children and she would cover my expenses. I thought that this was very kind of her.

We agreed to meet on Friday afternoon and she gave me £5 for my transport home. That £5 was like £5,000 to me and I left the meeting with Geraldine and God by my side.

Mama Bose and her lovely family taken around 1977. She was instrumental in saving me and my family at my lowest point.

When I got back to Mama Bose's house I told her excitedly that I had been offered a job at £10 per month and asked her if she would look after my children for £3 for the first 3 days while I was away. She agreed to this. Actually, I hadn't been offered the job definitely and hadn't been given any indication of what was entailed and how much I would be paid, but I had to tell Mama Bose something to get the ball rolling. Mama Bose was very encouraging and agreed to help me saying, "This may be your big chance, take it."

I also mentioned my intention to take a job in Lagos to Daddy Bose, Majekodum (Mama's husband) and he was not so convinced. He had been very helpful and kind to me over the years but appeared to know what I was now getting into. I learned later that he thought I was going to abandon my children, which was common amongst my age group at that time, but I had no intention of doing this—my children were very important to me and anything I did for myself was done equally for them.

As it happened I was using a young girl to help me with my children while I looked for work. She was called Maureen and had been introduced to me by a townsman called Innocent, who was her relative. She came from a very poor family, but seemed intelligent and honest so I had taken her on. When we first met she had said that I seemed to be too young for her to work for, and turned down my offer, so I got angry at what appeared to be an insult and walked away. However, A few weeks later Innocent told me that Maureen had gone to work for someone else but that these employers were abusive to her and she had left them. He said that she would now like to try working for me, and I agreed, although by then I would be finding it hard to employ anyone.

However, life became a bit easier. Maureen turned out to be a godsend (literally) and was like a second mother to my children and good companion for me. In fact I came to look upon her as a sister. She actually came from my village so we had much in common. The major problem had been the lack of money but we had managed to get by with such menial work as cleaning and washing dishes in Mama Bose's beer parlour, and collecting leftover food for ourselves and the children.

But now I was embarking on a new adventure and was happy that, at least, I had someone reliable to care for my children while I was away. Additionally Mama Bose would keep an eye on them all. But everything depended on a vague promise of work of unknown content with no guarantee of adequate recompense. A lot of people in Ijebu-Ode were now dependent on the outcome of this new venture.

On Friday afternoon I packed my few clothes and the only shoes I had at that time and went to meet Agnes at the agreed location. I was surprised to see her looking so glamorous and wearing what I can only describe as a 'Christmas dress'.

I felt a bit embarrassed with my clothes, but she said, "Don't worry, we'll sort you out when we get to Lagos."

We caught the luxury express bus to Lagos and during the 2 hour journey she told me something of what I would have to do. She said that she would take care of all the transport and hotel accommodation on condition that I paid her something if my 'luck shone'.

I still didn't understand what this was leading up to and was unsure whether I would be able to match up to her expectations. She sensed this and told me not to worry as she had made up her mind to help me.

She said, "I am sure you will be a success as you are prettier than me, and if I can do it you certainly can."

I was gradually getting the message but still didn't think I would be able to make the money she was indicating I would get. In fact I thought it was going to end with me being deep in debt and returning to Ijebu-Ode worse off than I had been before.

We arrived at Lagos bus station and took a taxi to a hotel called The Bayswater, directly opposite the Airport Hotel, in Ikeja, Lagos. The cost per night was £65 plus £200 deposit. Agnes paid for 3 nights and we were shown a double room with 2 big beds, beautifully made up. On entering this room I suddenly felt different; I had never experienced such luxury and a transformation came over me which I couldn't comprehend. I was being introduced to a new lifestyle and I felt overwhelmed. However, I was still not sure how I would be able to make enough money to pay Agnes back and suggested to her that we should perhaps find a cheaper place.

She told me that she had her reasons for choosing this hotel, and that anyone would be happy to pay for this. Anyway, we needed good security which the Bayswater provides

We had checked in at 7pm on November 10th 1975, I remember this moment as it was the moment my life was suddenly transformed. It is unforgettable since it held the key to a new beginning in my life. Agnes interrupted my thoughts by saying that we had to have a bath and get some rest before 11pm when we must be ready to go out. She seemed sure of what she was saying, but I couldn't see why going out so late was going to be important.

I questioned her on this and she replied firmly, "OK, I'll tell you everything and you must promise not to speak about it to anyone back in Ijebu-ode because nobody there knows what I do when I come here. I have invited you to join me as you seemed desperate enough to do any job. But you must zip your mouth when you go back."

"Our business is to go out and find white men, only white men, as there are no comebacks, and they pay well. I am giving you one of the keys to our room and if you find a white man you can bring him back for a short time, say one hour, and charge him £150. If he wants to stay all night it is £300. But of course if you are desirable to him they may pay much more. It's up to you to charge what you feel is right."

She then gave me a packet of condoms which I had to make absolutely sure the man used. "Remember, never do anything without one of these".

I asked her, "How could anybody pay such money; what do I have to do for it?"

She said, "You have to find out from them. They will tell you what they want. You said you would do any job and that is why I brought you here. You are a very pretty girl compared with the girls out there." She indicated towards the window. "So you should have no difficulty if you do exactly as I've told you."

She then went on, "I will not be able to take you into the Pecina (The Airport Hotel nightclub) because it costs £25 to get in and I have used up all my money on the hotel room. Hang around on the road and watch what the others are doing and I will come out from time to time to see how you are getting on."

"Now we must get some sleep. Wake me at 10pm."

I washed and lay down but I couldn't sleep; the excitement of the room was too much for me to waste on sleep, so I lay there with the thoughts of all that had happened racing through my head. I couldn't believe it was real and yet this was only the start.

At about 10pm I woke Agnes, as she had requested, and she told me that we should dress and make up. When I had finished what I thought would be suitable she said, "No, we'll have to do better than that," and told me to take my dress off and try on one of hers. Luckily we were the same size and it fitted perfectly. Then she told me to try her shoes and lent me some make-up.

I was now looking really good and Agnes said, "Ok, we're ready to go."

We went downstairs, through the foyer and out into the night. I felt excited as Agnes led me across the road to the Pecina night club. There was music in the air and people everywhere, mingling, talking and laughing. Of course I felt nervous but I was here to improve my situation and told myself to be strong and do what Agnes had said.

She then told me where to position myself and went into the Pecina. I just stood there and watched the other girls in action as Agnes had said I should. It was intriguing to see how they operated, first standing elegantly, and then moving provocatively to try and entice the men to go with them.

As I was watching them an older lady came up to me and said in a friendly manner, "I haven't seen you before, where are you from?"

"From Ijebu-Ode"

To which she responded, "Oh, that's a tough place. Isn't there lots of black magic there?"

I knew what she meant as it was a well-known centre for the carrying out of ritual ceremonies; human sacrifices where people, usually young girls, were invited or kidnapped and used as offerings in all kinds of rituals, usually for personal feuds or gain. In fact I had nearly been caught twice. Once when I was taking my baby to hospital, and I had been followed by a man who was eventually frightened off by the hospital authorities, and another time when a man had invited me to a hotel and I had managed to escape from his room after two other men came in carrying a rope.

I told her my story, adding that I was new to this game, and she became very motherly, saying that her name was Adani and that she would look after me, as part of her work for the other girls.

At that moment a car came through the main gate and stopped near to us. The driver, a white man, looked out of the car at me.

Adani said, "Quick, he's looking at you, go over before you lose him."

I couldn't move, not believing that I, a simple country girl, could be of interest to this man in his big flashy car. Suddenly the other girls were pushing past me to get to him but he wound up his window so they couldn't talk to him. After a minute he got out of his car and walked back to where I was standing.

He said casually, "Hello, can we talk."

I replied, somewhat shakily, "Yes," and we walked back to his car where he opened the passenger door for me.

Adani had followed us and was urging me to keep up with him.

"Quick, get into the car and talk to him, otherwise the other girls will snatch him away."

I was quite worried at what was happening, but Adani pushed me towards the car door, saying," You are very lucky. He is a good man."

So I got in and sat down next to him wondering what was going to happen next.

I needn't have worried as he moved up close and put his arm round me. He didn't do it in a rough way and I felt pleasantly relaxed and re-assured.

"Where do you live?" he said,

"In the hotel, just across the road."

He seemed surprised and said, "Can I come over with you?"

"OK", was all I could say, and he drove us over to the Hotel car park.

We went up to the room. The man, whose name was Harry seemed very pleased. It appeared to me that he wasn't expecting this, and asked me if there was room service.

Not knowing what he meant I said, "I don't know".

So he said he would find out and made a phone call to someone. He asked me what I would like and ordered drinks for us both. We quickly got to know each other, and I felt very comfortable with him. Although I had had very little contact with white people I could see he was an educated person with very good manners. After the drinks were brought and he had paid for them he asked me if I would join him for dinner the next evening at the Eko Holiday Inn. I told him that I had a friend with me and he said that that it would be good if she could come too. He would bring his friend also, and they might get on together.

We then had a bit of fun, after which he said, "What do I owe you?"

Not knowing what to say (I was too embarrassed to ask for £60 as Agnes had stipulated) I replied, "Whatever you wish."

He said, "This hotel must be costing you a fortune," and put a bundle of notes on the table.

He then gave me his phone number so I could call him to confirm our date for the next evening. I picked up the money without counting it and hid it behind the dressing table. It looked a lot more than £60. We went out. I locked the room door and followed him downstairs and across to the Airport Hotel.

He said that he would collect us the next evening if I rang him to confirm our meeting and I promised that I would. Then he kissed me goodnight, went to his car, and was gone.

I really couldn't believe it had all happened and stood there for some time, collecting my thoughts. I vaguely noticed that cars were moving past slowly, and men were calling out. It was unreal and I had to force myself to move. I decided to look for Agnes but I found out from one of the other girls that she was still in the night club. As I had not brought the money that I had earned in the room I couldn't get into the club so I waited outside for her. Almost immediately a white man walked up to me and asked me if we could go somewhere.

Rather unnecessarily, I said, "Why?"

"Because I would like to spend some time with you," he replied.

I agreed and told him that we could go to my hotel. He said we could go in his car and he drove the short distance back to the Bayswater. When we got there he seemed surprised and said, "Haven't you got a house? This is very expensive."

I said I was only staying there for a couple of days, so we went in and up to my room, had some fun and talked a lot. I told him some of my story which seemed to intrigue him. His name was Paul and he appeared to be very interested in me, adding that he would like to meet me again.

The whole picture was becoming much clearer to me. These were rich men with more money than they cared about. Paul gave me £200 and said that he would leave me to sleep as I didn't seem to be the type of girl who should be in this business. He arranged to come next day to pick me up and we could go and have lunch together before I went back to Ijebu-Ode. I accepted and he left me his phone number. He also took the hotel number so he could call me. Then he kissed me goodnight and made me promise not to go out anymore that night. I had made two appointments in 3 hours!

I locked the door and took the first bunch of notes from where I had hidden them and excitedly counted it—£260! I couldn't begin to believe this was happening. I had 'earned' £460 without even trying—at last God was giving something back to me. I danced and jumped all round the room in my excitement. I really couldn't sleep in this state so I hid the money, in the bathroom this time, after taking £20, and went out to find Agnes.

Returning to the Airport Hotel I paid to get into the night club and found Agnes at a table with some white men. She was very pleased that I had come as she had been worried that one of the men she was with would be snatched away by other girls. Now that I was there she could get me to keep him at her table. She had already told him that she had a friend for him and I had arrived just in time. There was no spare seat, so the man got up, offered me his, and went to find another one. I thought this was very kind of him.

The night continued with dancing, good music and drinks up to 3:30 am. I asked Agnes if her man would pay for her just to dance with him and she said, "No, I am going to his house with him and you can ask your man if he is going to take you home."

I was surprised at this and said, "We can't because we have this lovely room in the hotel which we have paid for. How can we leave it empty?"

Agnes seemed irritated at my continual questioning and explained wearily that we had to make enough money to pay for that place.

She said, "If you like you can go and sleep there, but tomorrow you have to contribute to the cost of it."

How I looked when I started my new career in Lagos aged 22.

Because we were all together, and Agnes was dancing or talking with her man, I couldn't tell her that I already had enough to pay for everything myself. So I just sat with the man she had found for me while we talked. In fact he did all the talking which suited me as I was not used to this new environment. In the end he asked me to go home with him at about 4 am. It turned out that both men lived in the same house. We entertained them and left their place in the morning at about 10:30. As I was getting into the taxi my man asked me if I would be his permanent girlfriend as he had become highly interested in me, so we arranged that we would meet the following weekend.

When Agnes and I arrived back at our hotel I could at last talk to her about my experiences during the previous evening. I told her what I had made from the first man and the other man I had met before she saw me in the Pecina, and showed her the money I had hidden in the room. She was astonished and, to be honest, I was too. I offered her £1000 for my contribution to our expenses and at first she wouldn't take it, but I insisted. She must have thought I was an expert at this business rather than someone just starting out. I had already worked out that her method of sitting in the Pecina with one client was not the way to make 'big' money. Her style was the 'upper class' method whereas I could see that it was possible to make much more by dealing with many men outside. There was really no difference in the 'class' of man (inside or outside) but the takings were hugely different. Agnes was more comfortable with her system so I didn't push it with her. Perhaps she would see the light when she saw what I had lined up for us.

I told her that we had been invited to dinner that evening, to which she replied, "You know that today is Saturday and that is the big day for our kind of stuff. We should be able to double what we made last night. Why don't you call your man and suggest that we see them earlier and then we can be back here before midnight for the evening work?"

I saw the sense in that and rang Harry to agree a time for our date. He said that would be fine and he would send a car to pick us up. This impressed Agnes who said they must be rich and worth getting to know.

We now had time to get some rest and, anyway, I wanted to go out, do some shopping and get my hair permed. By the time the car arrived I was looking very elegant and much more confident than I had been the day before. I was getting the hang of my new career and didn't want to waste any time.

The car took us to a restaurant where Harry and his friend were waiting for us at the bar. Agnes seemed very impressed with them and I think she was starting to take more notice of my business sense and taste in clients. After dinner we all went to one of the top nightclubs in Lagos and during the evening it became obvious that Agnes had abandoned all ideas of going back to the Pecina. This was far above what she had been used to and we spent the rest of day enjoying the good life with our friends.

At about midnight Harry suggested to us that we spend the night with them at their house, which we did. The next morning he said that we were all getting on so well that Agnes and I should check out of the Bayswater and come back to their house for the rest of the weekend. He drove us there and we got our belongings. We would have checked out anyway as we had intended to return to Ijebu-Ode on Sunday evening. Agnes had to be back for her 'day job'. We then returned to the house for the rest of the day, entertaining and being entertained by our friends. It was a lifestyle I could get used to.

Later in the afternoon Agnes told the men that she had to leave to go to another town that evening and I said I would also have to go. They were a bit disappointed but said that as they'd enjoyed themselves so much we should meet every weekend. Before we left they paid us—Agnes got £1000 and I received £1500. Then we told them not to bother driving us—we would get a taxi back into town ourselves.

On the journey back into Lagos Agnes and I discussed our immediate plans. As I had made a few appointments for the following week it was agreed that I would stay in Lagos after Agnes had left. I suggested that I should give her £1000 to give to Mama Bose and Maureen to make sure my children were alright.

She was horrified and said, "You can't give them that, they'll wonder what you've been doing. I'll give Mama Bose £20 and make sure that they don't run short."

With so much money I was beginning to lose touch with the reality of life back home

After Agnes had gone I booked myself back into the Bayswater and then remembered that I'd arranged to meet Paul on Saturday, so I gave him a call to apologise. I told him that I'd had to go out of town unexpectedly but could see him in the evening. He was very good about it and declined politely saying that he had an early start on Monday. He added that he was sure he'd see me again.

I was on my own and, now that I knew what I was doing, got dressed, made up and went down on to road. I had a couple of short times, using the hotel room, and after the second time met the old madam, Adani, who remarked admiringly, "Yes girl, you've certainly got the gist of it now—I can see you're a true Ijebu girl. You move like an eagle, down on to your prey and away."

I replied, "I thank God for that. Opportunity does not come often to me, but when it does I take it."

It may not have been acceptable to some but the circumstances of my life had forced this on me and nothing was going to come between me and success. Especially now that God had finally intervened to save the lives of my children.

CHAPTER 15

Finding the Rainbow

I worked twice as fast as the other girls. One thing Agnes had been right about was the use of the Bayswater Hotel. The others wasted a lot of time by not having somewhere to base themselves and the increase in business easily covered the extra cost. Most of them lived in Lagos and hadn't worked it out for themselves, thinking only of the high cost of a room which, to them, seemed unnecessary. The money I was making never ceased to astonish me and I made sure that Adani was well rewarded for helping. She was a lovely old woman and became another mother to me. I often think of her to this day and how she had protected and advised me during those first frantic evenings when I was at my most vulnerable.

I did see Paul again and got to know him well. He worked for a German construction company and invited me to live with him outside Lagos. He seemed very serious about me but I was more interested in getting the maximum out of this business, which meant having a wide client supply. I really wanted to make as much as I could while it lasted. I also had to return to Ijebu-ode periodically, to visit my children, and I began to realise that it would be more advantageous to live in Lagos with my helper Maureen and the children. However, this would require me finding my own house or flat away from my 'workplace' so I could separate my two lifestyles. I didn't want to live with Paul as I had to keep the men I was dealing with separate from each other. Before I could work out how to do this a development occurred which seemed to solve my predicament.

One evening I was sitting in the Pecina night club when a large group of white men came in. They were led by a huge fat man who was talking very loudly and appearing to be organising a party.

He saw me sitting on my own and came over, saying in a very jolly way, "Hi, young lady, may we join you?"

"Yes, it's my pleasure." I replied, in my poshest accent.

He and the others then started pulling tables together and while this was going on the fat man, his name was Mike, came over to me and asked, "D'you think you could arrange for some lovely ladies like you to come and join me and my boys?"

I smiled at him, "Yes, that'll be easy", and, looking very efficient, called over to a girl I knew, Helen, to get some girls in. She went out and came back in with a crowd. However, she tried to get one of her friends partnered with Mike and suggested to me that I sit with a particularly ugly man. I hadn't been accepted into her circle yet.

Mike saw what was happening and, gesticulating wildly, shouted at Helen, "Oh no, that's my baby, she sits with me!"

Helen got her just desserts by finally finishing up with the ugly man herself. My luck was in again.

She was still thinking about the business, though, and, when she managed to speak to me, out of Mike's earshot, told me to make sure that I ordered large gin and tonics for myself and she would make sure that the barman produced water and lemon. She said that this is what all the girls did and they would split the takings with the barman later. I had learnt another trick of the trade.

As the evening wore on and Mike and his 'boys' got progressively merrier I began to get restless at the thought of the business I was losing outside. This was Agnes's policy of one man in the comfortable surroundings of the nightclub and I didn't like it. However, I had to accept the situation since I was in at the start and Mike was all over me. Then at 4am, the party began to break up. Mike was sloshed and, staggering as he got up, slurred, "Honey, you're going to have to get me to my room."

He said he was in the penthouse suite in the Airport Hotel across the road so, with some help from his friends, I got him to his feet and walked him over to the entrance. Once inside he was manoeuvred into the lift with me. Helen, who had come to the lift with us whispered, "Make sure you're out of his room by 6am, it's the rules. And get all the loose change out of his pocket, he won't remember what he had."

Then I was on my own with this huge man. The lift stopped at the top floor and we struggled out and down the corridor to his door. Luckily he could just about stay on his feet and get the key into the lock. Once inside he made straight for the bed and flopped down telling me to get his shoes and trousers off. I wondered if he was going to be capable of anything other than falling unconscious, as his trousers came off, money falling out all over the place. He gave up trying to continue and fell back on the bed, half undressed, snoring almost immediately. Remembering what Helen had told me I started picking up the money and putting it into my bag. I was worried that Mike might wake up and catch me but he was too far gone and, in any case, I could do what I liked as long as I could hear his snoring which was increasing in intensity.

I had a look round the suite. It was massive with several rooms, like a palace to me and far above what I had thought was the luxury of my hotel room. Then I went into the bathroom to use the toilet and noticed a large case which was half open on the floor. I lifted the lid and was astonished to see it was neatly packed with wads of banknotes. I thought I was dreaming and all sorts of wild thoughts ran through my head. This was too much for me to comprehend and I tried to think rationally of what to do. The closest I had been to this much money was when the victorious Nigerian army were dishing out money to the Biafrans at the end of the war. But that was nothing compared to what I was looking at now and the temptation to help myself caught me in its grip. I could live the rest of my life without any more worries on this—surely God had placed me in this position for a reason. But he was going far beyond my simple request for help, made only a week ago.

After a few moments sanity returned and I realised that there was no way I could make off with this, despite Helen's insistence that any loose change Mike had on his person was fair game. Loose change!! What would Helen have thought of this? I did think of throwing some of it out of the window and racing downstairs to pick it up, but luckily I dismissed that idea as too risky, for many reasons. I obviously couldn't openly carry much downstairs and past reception, so I settled on stuffing as much as I could into my tiny handbag.

As I came out of the bathroom Mike, who had been snoring continuously since falling asleep on top of the bed, turned over and coughed. He stopped snoring and I was convinced he was about to wake and catch me. I was petrified and thought of lying next him until he was snoring again, but I couldn't do it. Then I decided on a different tack. I would shake him and say that, as it was late, I had to go hoping that he would think I had been next to him all the time. When I did this he turned to look at me with unseeing eyes and muttered how sorry he was for his condition and that he would see me that evening. I thankfully got out of his place, quickly took the lift to the ground floor, cleared reception, and stumbled out into the breaking dawn.

Back in my room I counted the money from the whole evening. I was getting used to it and the earlier feelings of excitement had receded. Then I tried to rest, but I couldn't sleep properly so I went out again and did some shopping. In the afternoon I went to see Helen. I told her what had happened and she said I had hit the jackpot. She told me that Mike was a company director from England who visited his Lagos factory every 6 months to meet clients and take his expatriate workers out on the town as a reward for their good work. I said that I didn't want to meet him again in case he'd noticed the missing money and then I'd be in trouble.

Taken during my work in Lagos, aged 23.

Helen was emphatic that this was the last thing I should do. "It will make things worse. You are one of us and if you don't appear tonight it will look even more suspicious. You must be there. He won't notice it anyway, it's peanuts to him."

So I went to the Pecina at about 8pm feeling very tense. Mike was already there, surrounded by girls. He was demanding to know where I was.

He turned and saw me, saying in his loud voice, "Ah, there's my girl, where have you been?" He pushed his way through the girls and hugged me tightly, then gesturing to a table, said, "Come over here and have a drink with me."

We sat down and he started talking about how much he'd enjoyed himself last night, and how he wanted to know all about me. After a couple of drinks he said, "We can't talk here, let's go to my room."

So we went up to his penthouse, this time in a much more orderly manner than before. He opened the door and ushered me in. It didn't seem long since I had been there and I wondered if he'd noticed anything missing from the night before. So far, it seemed he hadn't.

We made ourselves comfortable on the sofa and he sat close to me saying, "OK, tell me all about yourself; I have a feeling that you are a very interesting girl."

So I recounted my story from the beginning. I have always found that people seem to find most aspects of my life interesting and this was certainly the case with Mike who, when I had finished, sat up and said admiringly, "That is some journey for a young girl, you deserve to be rewarded and I'm going to do exactly that."

He didn't explain further what he meant. Instead he said that he wanted to relax with me first. So, for a couple of hours, we got to know each other a bit better.

Later, he began to explain what he had in mind. He started by saying that I should find somewhere nice to live in Lagos. "It's a waste to be cooped up in a hotel, so I want you to rent a house. When you've found somewhere you like, give me a call and we'll look it over and I'll put it on the books if it's good enough for us."

It was now getting late and Mike said he didn't want to go out on the town again. He said I was welcome to stay with him till the morning.

As I was quite tired, and emotionally relieved that he apparently had no knowledge of the missing money, I accepted and we slept together in the huge bed.

I woke, refreshed, at about 8am and quickly got up, washed, did myself up, and left before Mike had stirred. I was excited about what he had said and had decided to consult Helen on what I should do. She was astonished when I told her what had happened and said that I should act quickly before he changed his mind.

She warned me, "Men are always promising things to us girls to get something quick and then conveniently forgetting the promise until they need us again."

I hadn't thought of this aspect, as Mike had seemed so genuine, and it brought me down to earth.

Anyway, Helen was still talking, "I know a landlord called Alahaji in Akeja who might be able to find somewhere for me, we'll go and see him straight away."

I was in luck as Alahaji said that he had a bungalow which a German expatriate had just vacated.

He said, "You'd better look at it now. If you're ready I'll drive you over."

So we got in his car and when we arrived I was very impressed. It was in a very select area and had a beautiful garden. I told Alahaji to book it for me and I would get my client to come round and finalise the agreement.

He looked at me knowingly, obviously very familiar with this sort of arrangement.

"No problem," he smiled, "Tell him it's £350 per month."

I rushed back excitedly to Mike's hotel to give him the information before he had time to change his mind. We then drove to the house and he agreed that it would suit us perfectly.

"I'll take it on for 3 years initially, is that ok with you?" He said in a businesslike manner.

I tried to look casual and replied, "Oh yes that'll be fine, it's certainly a lot more comfortable than the hotel."

Then we went to Alahaji and, to my astonishment, Mike paid up fully for 3 years rent. He seemed childishly pleased at this arrangement and added that we should go to FFF (The main furniture supplier in Lagos) to arrange for an entire replacement of all furnishings. He also said that he would arrange for all the interior decoration and fittings, including a telephone, to be carried out and that I should be able to move in by the end of the week. Then he told me that he would be leaving on Thursday and after he had gone I should stop working. He would make sure that I had everything and it would all be covered by his office.

Things were happening to me so fast that I had to pinch myself in case I was dreaming, but it wasn't a dream and I had to slow down so I could gather my thoughts. I spent a couple of nights with Mike and then went to see him off at the airport. When I got back to the bungalow the new phone rang and it was him telling me how much he'd enjoyed my company and to promise that I would be a good girl while he was away. He said that he would be in touch from time to time and would see me on his next visit. I was his girl!

I did stop work but only because I had to get back to Ijebu-ode to see my children. In fact I would now be taking them and Maureen to their new home. But first I had to see Agnes to tell her what had happened since she had left Lagos. In fact I saw her just as she was getting ready to go to Lagos for the weekend.

She was surprised to see me, saying, "Why are you back so early? I thought you would have stayed longer, what with all the commitments you had."

When I told her, she was speechless. I don't think she fully believed me, saying, "It takes girls years, if ever, to land the big one. But I've seen you in action and it must be true."

I said, proudly, "When you get to Lagos you'll be staying in my place." She laughed and told me I was a 'one in a million girl'.

Then I went to see Mama Bose who said that she hardly recognised me in my big town outfit. She thanked me for the money I had sent her through Agnes and then I told her that I would be taking Maureen and the children to live with me in Lagos.

All she could say was, "I knew you could do it. When I first saw you I knew you were special."

CHAPTER 16

The Man from Skibbereen

I was seeing Paul on a regular basis now. The routine was that he would pick me up from the airport hotel. I didn't want him to know about the arrangement with Mike. Anyway, Mike was fat, and far worse, he was married. But he had set me up and I had to keep him happy. He only visited Lagos once every 6 months which suited my purposes perfectly. However, on his next visit he didn't make contact with me. Then, a few days after his arrival, I met one of his employees, who looked at me strangely.

"You've been a naughty girl, haven't you?" he said, admonishingly
. I immediately knew what this meant. I had had a couple of arrangements with his workers while Mike was away. It was more flirting than anything, but he had interpreted what he'd been told as something more than this, so I sensed that my life style was about to change again.

One of Mike's secretaries eventually called and told me that I'd messed up 'big time' and he wouldn't be having anything more to do with me. That was it, short and to the point. So I began to remove my possessions from the house before I was thrown out. I asked Paul to help me move and when he saw where I'd been living he was astonished. He then realised that I wasn't the common girl that he'd thought I was, and became very much more interested in me.

Not long after this Paul was transferred to Medugri in the North and he suggested that I and the children move there with him, which I did. I was very happy with this period of my life and we lived as man and wife for 2 years until I decided that I wanted a house built for my children in my home village of Nguru Mbaise. My father's house was falling down and Paul agreed to help with the financing after which we planned to visit Germany. We would settle there permanently if I found I liked it.

I subsequently received word that the re-building of my father's house was approaching completion and I made plans to visit Nguru to finalise the arrangements for my children. However, when I arrived I found that the work on the house was far from complete and the money we had sent was gone. To complicate matters an uncle died while I was there and I became involved with the funeral arrangements.

Paul, meanwhile, had booked flights for us to go to Germany but I was so deeply involved with the events in Nguru that I found I couldn't make the date. I was unable to get a message to him in order to warn him of the situation. I tried to contact him to no avail so, in the end, I just didn't turn up for the flight. I finally managed to get away some weeks later and left the children, and what money remained, with Jemima. When I finally got back to Lagos I found that Paul had left without leaving any message for me. I assumed that he was angry at my 'no show' and had flown off alone. Since this was just another typical occurrence in my eventful life I accepted it and wasted no time in renting a room in a Lagos hostel where the other working girls I knew were living.

Once again I was penniless and resumed my trade to try and get myself together again. This was a shock to my system as I had become used to a comfortable life but, here I was, starting out again. Nevertheless, I was used to these knocks and just got on with it.

One evening, a couple of months later, I was standing in my working position on the street when an old man with long white hair and a wispy beard came out of the Nitel building, where the public could make International telephone calls. I was intrigued by his appearance as I had always liked older men—a throwback to my love of my grandfathers.

I went over to him and said, "Hullo sir" in my professional voice.

"Hullo yourself, young lady," he replied in a surprisingly deep and educated English accent.

I went on, "I like you; can we have a chat?"

He laughed in the manner that men in this position did when they knew nothing would progress beyond this point. "And what should we chat about?" he enquired, politely.

I grabbed his arm, pulled him to a parked car and pushed him up against it. He looked startled. Men are always surprised at my strength in comparison with my small stature. I enjoy it immensely when they discover I'm not a weak and feeble woman, and this man was no different.

Then he recovered himself and, laughing nervously, exclaimed, "Lady, you're too young for me—I'm too old for you. But you are very beautiful!"

I responded quickly with, "Beauty is nothing, but character is needed."

He seemed to like that and became relaxed. We introduced ourselves, his name was Lister which intrigued me more since I had not come across this name before. He asked me if I would like to accompany him into the Pecina and we went in together after he had paid for us both. He led me to a table where a man and a woman were seated. He introduced me to the man who was called Bob and I said that I already knew his friend—Bena. She also lived in the hostel.

We chatted and enjoyed ourselves immensely for a few hours. These men were my perfect types—sophisticated and worldly wise. Finally Lister suggested that I come back to his house where Bob, who was from out of town, was staying as his guest. Bena was invited along as well. So we all went and as it happened, stayed the night.

The next day Bob said that he had to return to his work at Ife which was a day's drive away, but that he would be very happy if we all joined him. Bena and I jumped at this and we got a taxi back to the hostel to collect some things for our 'holiday'. When we returned Lister and Bob were ready to leave and our bags were packed in Lister's car. This car was a Citroen and had suspension which rose when the car was started. I sat in the passenger seat next to Lister—it was huge and I felt like royalty.

The journey took all day but we eventually arrived at Bob's bungalow in Ife. This was a great new experience for me as I couldn't get over the quality of these men compared to most of those I had associated with. We settled in and had a meal and some drinks. Everything was perfect and I felt that I was starting another phase in my life. How right I was!!

Bob's work in Ife took him away next day leaving Lister, Bena and me to amuse ourselves. I noticed that Lister and Bena were smoking marijuana which I had never tried or even felt like trying. However, they said that I should really see what I was missing and managed to persuade me to give it a go. I did smoke ordinary cigarettes so I knew how to inhale. But after a couple of puffs of this stuff I was overcome. I remember laughing uncontrollably until my sides ached and then I collapsed unconscious. I had fallen asleep at midday and didn't wake until next morning.

Bob had returned the previous evening and had wondered why I was not around. He had laughed when Lister and Bena told him what had happened but I think he was a bit concerned for me since he didn't smoke this 'stuff' himself. I eventually woke with very little recollection of what had happened to me. I still smoke today (Benson and Hedges Gold—nothing else) but I have never touched any drug since that day.

A few days later Lister and I returned to Lagos leaving Bob and Bena in Ife. On the drive back we spoke continuously the whole way. I adore conversation and here was a man who could talk with passion. It was meat and drink to my demanding character; similar to my appetite for education. I couldn't get enough of it. We discovered all about ourselves. Lister was a Professor of Psychology and said he was fascinated to know more about me and why I was living the way I did.

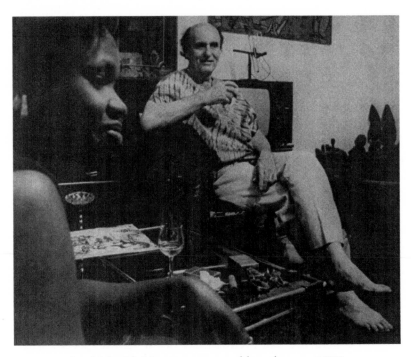

Aged 24 with Lister in my rented hostel room, 1977.

I told him my whole story and he hardly spoke while I recounted everything from my birth to the moment I met him. He was quite overcome at times and I have the same problem when I re-live my story. That is why I don't often recall things in my past. I don't forget anything but the pain is too much and my memories are too vivid.

When we arrived at Lagos we both felt drained and after Lister had dropped me off at the hostel I lay on my bed, exhausted, and fell into a deep sleep. The second total coma, in as few days, but for a very different reason. I had been mesmerised by an encounter with an extraordinary human being.

I saw a lot of Lister after that, mostly in bars and clubs, and we had much fun together. One evening I invited him into my room. This triggered off another psychological jolt in me. On my bed was a book I had been reading. It was called 'The Man from Skibbereen'. I had started to read it purely because of the name 'Skibbereen'. This was the village in Ireland that my father had told me so much about. He had lived in the area after the war and had promised that he would send me to Ireland when I was older for further education. I had never forgotten that name and, since my father died before he could fulfil his promise to me, I had given up ever seeing this place. As a growing child I had imagined that Ireland was in heaven and that was where my parents were. The closest I had got to it was in this book which I had found lying on a table in a bar.

Lister saw the book and became very animated.

"Good God, I am the man from Skibbereen. This is unbelievable! Do you know that I have a big house which is on a hill overlooking Skibbereen?"

I felt the excitement running through us both. This was a mystical turn of events. The chances of this man seeing the name of a place embedded in my mind and for him to also be the man from this place, was too much to take in.

We both sat down on my bed. This was the moment I truly started loving Lister.

He said, quietly, "Would you like me to take you there?"

I couldn't answer as the tears were rolling down my face. When something makes me cry it takes me over and I cannot control my emotions. It is the same thing—opposite ends of the spectrum—great anger and, best of all, great joy.

I had been struck by the most powerful force of my turbulent life and knew that this was the pinnacle of that powerful force. It was as though I had met my father and that he was, at last, going to take me to the place of my dreams.

My life was about to change in a way that dwarfed all that had gone before. At that moment I couldn't comprehend what was about to happen to me. It is just as well that we don't know the future. I would probably have died of happiness, unable to take it all in at once. The most interesting part of my life was about to unfold.

Significant Events and Facts relating to the Biafran War July 1967—January 1970:

— Nigeria was granted independence from UK in October 1960.

— 1964 General Election held which was not considered to be free or fair by many.

— Nigeria's Prime Minister killed in a coup staged in January 1966.

— In May 1966 there were riots in the North and Easterners living there were attacked.

— General Gowon was declared head of the Nigerian Federal Military Government (effectively Head of State) after a counter coup by Northern army units in July 1966.

— By September 1966 many thousands of Igbo living in the North had been killed or forced to flee back to the East. Some Northerners living in the East were killed in reprisals.

— Eastern and Northern troops were moved back into their own territories in January 1967.

— After a peace meeting in January 1967 held in Ghana, Col Ojukwu, the Eastern regional governer, declared Eastern Nigeria to be the Independent State of Biafra. (30th May 1967)

— July 1967 Outbreak of Civil War

— Four phases were planned by the Federal Government in order to annex Eastern Nigeria (Biafra):

1. Capture of Nsukka,
2. Capture of Ogoja,
3. Capture of Abakaliki,
4. Capture of Enugu.

— Nigeria blockaded sea routes into Biafra to deny supplies.

— Biafran army was mainly funded by the Biafran civilian population.

— Biafran women and young people were called up for spying duties in order to gather information on positions and strengths of Nigerian forces.

— **1967 Irene Chioma Opariji (aged 13) joined the Biafran Buffs (Intelligence)**

— Nigeria also recruited intelligence gatherers and people often changed sides to suit their situation.

— Biafra was too small to go on the offensive so fought a defensive, guerrilla style war together with a bombing campaign on major towns.

— Some foreign mercenaries were employed by Biafra.

— The town of Enugu was considered to be the symbol of independence from Nigeria.

— In 1968 Enugu and Port Harcourt were captured by Nigerian forces.

— In early 1969 Nigerian forces were advancing on Owerri.

— **October 1969 Irene Chioma Opariji (aged 15) left the Biafran Army**

— Biafra put up stiff resistance to try and hold off the advance using guerrilla tactics but were eventually overwhelmed and Owerri fell in December 1969.

— In January 1970 Head of the State of Biafra, Col. Ojukwu and his family, flew out of Biafra as the situation became hopeless. He handed over the Biafran army to General Effiong who surrendered to Gen Gowon. (12th January 1970)

— General Gowon says in a speech to the defeated Biafrans:

"The Federal Government has mounted massive relief operations to alleviate the suffering of the people in the newly liberated areas. We are mobilising adequate resources to provide food, shelter, and medicines for the affected population. My government has directed that former civil servants and public corporation officials should be promptly reinstated as they come out of hiding. Details of this exercise have been published. Plans for the rehabilitation of self—employed people will also be announced promptly. We have overcome a lot over the past four years. I have therefore every confidence that ours will become a great nation".

It is estimated that, at least, one million people died during the conflict, either from the effects of battle or from side effects such as starvation.

ABOUT THE AUTHOR

Chioma was born into the affluent Oparaji family of high status, the last of nine children and the only girl. She should have been assured of a comfortable and loving upbringing surrounded by the extended family of cousins, aunts, uncles and grandparents, traditionally living together in the family compound in the village of Ezuhu Nguru, Eastern Nigeria. Instead, cruelly orphaned and being much younger than her brothers, she existed at subsistence level throughout the early years of her childhood eventually escaping from the status of child witch at the age of 13 to take part in the Biafran War. Subsequently she returned to the struggle for survival in post-war Biafra and with a growing family of her own was, at the age of 21 ready to transform her life.

In 1986 she decided to move her family to England which she considered the ideal place to further her lifestyle and the education of her 5 children. This was against the strong advice of her husband. In some ways this was a good idea and in others it was a disaster and she was repeatedly thrown back into the struggles of her past. The worst was the ending of the marriage to her golden man—he couldn't face London and returned to his other love, Africa. She now lives in Brixton, London and this year has been chosen as a London Ambassador for the 2012 Olympic Games. She has much more to give, tirelessly working for her charity 'Ladies of Substance', an organisation dedicated to helping black families lost in the turbulence of inner city London with its racial undertones and gang culture.

Lightning Source UK Ltd.
Milton Keynes UK
UKOW042121021212

203063UK00002B/48/P